THE ULTIMATE HEALING

Living With Cancer

Ken Farnsworth

MOREHOUSE PUBLISHING
WILTON, CONNECTICUT

Morehouse Publishing
78 Danbury Road
Wilton, Connecticut 06897

The bible text in this book is from the Revised Standard Version, © 1946,
1952, 1971, by the Division of Christian Education of the National
Council of Churches of Christ in the United States of America. Used by
permission.

Library of Congress Cataloging-in-Publication Data
    1. Farnsworth, Ken—Health. 2. Cancer—Patients—California—
Biography. 3. Christian life—1960-   I. Title.
RC265.6.F37A3   1989
362.1'96994'0092—dc20
[B] 89-8285 CIP

ISBN: 0-8192-1482-5

Cover design by Carole Masonberg.
Cover photography by J. Tesson/H. Armstrong Roberts, Inc.

Printed in the United States of America
by
BSC LITHO,
Harrisburg, PA

To the memories of Kenneth, my father, and Alice and Martha, my sisters, all of whom prematurely succumbed to cancer many years ago—and to my mother, Mable, who loved them.

Three times I besought the Lord about this, that it should leave me; but he said to me, 'My grace is sufficient for you, for my power is made perfect in weakness.'

2 Cor. 12:8, 9

Contents

Introduction

Imagine sitting in one of those cold, sterile examining rooms presently in vogue in doctors' offices. You have endured three weeks of tests and evaluations. Now, you are perched on the examining table—the kind with a continuous roll of paper that is replaced after each patient by pulling down a new section and tearing off the old. You may be wondering whether the nurse did this before you entered the room.

After a fifteen-minute wait that seems like two hours, your doctor enters the room. "We don't have good news," he says soberly. "You have a mass in the area of your left kidney. We think it is malignant. We won't know for sure what it is until we get in there. With proper treatment you may have two years left."

How do you react? What goes on in your mind with this pronouncement of certain death? How do you cope?

This work is an extension, a sequel, to the story told in *Journey to Healing,* published by CBP Press in 1985. The Christian Board of Publication in St. Louis, Missouri, operates this publishing house.

Journey to Healing, relates an almost minute-by-minute account of my first bout with cancer. It begins with a visit to my family doctor in early 1983. It ends with my return to law practice ten months later after massive surgery, chemotherapy, and radiation therapy. I was then totally cancer-free. The entire adventure was, to me, a religious experience of more than mountaintop proportions.

It is now five years after the ordeal described in the first book. Because I have seen the inspiration *Journey to Healing* has been to cancer patients who have read it, I am led to share the years since that first experience.

There are dangers lurking to spoil an effort such as this, but my hopes are great. I hope that by sharing my continuing experience others who are undergoing some of these trials will find hope and strength. I do not want to oversimplify this message by creating a slogan, but there is no more simple way to put it. You can live with cancer. That's it.

That is it in a very small nutshell. It is not, of course, true in all cases. When cancer is discovered, the health of the patient, the type of medical care accepted by the patient, and the type of cancer are among many factors that determine the applicability of the statement.

Many books are readily available covering fatal or terminal illness. Many approaches are proffered. Some are spiritual, some medical, and many enlist the positive-thinking bromides of the New Age, currently so popular. There is much to be said for many of these, or a combination of several. When dealing with cancer, one cannot argue with "whatever works."

Several times I decided not to write this book. The last thing I want to convey is the idea that I sat down and conjured up a positive mental attitude and therefore am still here and in good health. A reading of *Journey to Healing* should dispel any such notion. I hope the facts shared with the reader in the pages to follow will show decidedly that the healing set forth in *Journey to Healing* and herein is a spiritual one, a gift from God.

God's healing gift is essentially the healing of your spirit. Various degrees of physical healing will certainly accompany it. The vital healing, in the last analysis, is a healing of the spirit. Once that has happened, you can live with cancer, or any other fatal disease, with a perspective that allows you, the patient, to accept your situation and be a convincing vessel of God's reality and love at the same time. It does not beg the question to say, "Everybody dies, sooner or later." But many times you do not have a gut realization of that fact until you have stared death in the eyes.

Cancer patients do this every day. Many cancers, properly treated, are not going to cause death anytime soon, if at all. Even so, the news that we have cancer is, until we find out otherwise, a death sentence. Our defenses go into play immediately. Fear is the most immobilizing response of all. For weeks and months after the initial diagnosis, this deadly emotion dictates our daily activities. Somehow, we must learn to defeat fear. How can we do that? If our fear of death can be defused, there is not much left to fear, is there?

This fear comes and goes. The fear that the disease will return after it has been healed, or has gone into remission, is essentially a part of the fear of death. It seems fair to say that most of our fears are components of the one ultimate fear—the fear of death.

The main purpose of *Journey to Healing* was to demonstrate how I found the Lord because of my cancer. It ended when I returned to work, having been pronounced well. The year 1983 was what I have called many times my "walk with God." The book ends with my beginning to pray in the Spirit as I was trying to give thanks to God for having brought me through the ordeal. Contrary to my own spiritual evaluation of myself at the time, I was a mere babe in the spiritual woods. I still am, though I can detect some growth in the last five years.

I hope that by sharing my spiritual and medical travels since *Journey to Healing* I can bring to cancer patients (I detest the term *cancer victim*) some methods and thoughts that will help them evaluate their positions. By doing this, the fear of death can be diluted, even dispatched. When that happens, the patient can make the very best use of whatever physical assets he or she has left—make the quality of the remaining life the very best possible. After all, that is what life should be all about, with or without cancer.

One man who has been of invaluable help in the writing of this book is the Reverend John Rollinson, vicar of the Episcopal Church of the Resurrection in Clovis, California. His advice and counsel throughout, on everything from punctuation to theology, has made the work involved a pleasant task. To him I give my deepest thanks.

Certainly, I make no apologies for the fact that the only sure way to such a state is through the total acceptance of

God through his Son, Jesus Christ. If acted upon, it opens all the doors. Come with me now through my last five years of living with cancer.

1. Conversion

[God] will wipe away every tear from their eyes, and death shall be no more, neither shall there be mourning nor crying nor pain any more, for the former things have passed away.

Rev. 21:4

What an experience! I had nothing with which to compare it. I was driving along the freeway after my final visit to Dr. Wittlinger, my oncologist. He was one of the doctors responsible for my being cancer-free on this late October day in 1983. He gave me my chemotherapy. Earlier in the day he told me I was well and that my treatment was complete.

Eight months before I had undergone massive surgery to remove a basketball-size tumor from my inferior vena cava. It was very malignant, a leiomyosarcoma, it was called. This simply means it was a cancer of the smooth-muscle tissue, in my case, the vena cava, which can be described as the main north-south vein in the body.

Without the surgery my remaining life was estimated in months. With it, some of the doctors were so optimistic as to give me two years. The intervening months were given to taking thirty-two radiation treatments, two herculean doses of powerful chemicals, and the formidable task of healing physically and getting back on my feet. Shortly after the operation I was told there was a chance I would not walk again due to the damage done to the vena cava and, hence, to my circulation.

By this great day, the day of my medical release, I was walking two miles a day with no problem. I was well. I could not yet fathom the spiritual dimension of the fact that I was healed of this terrible cancer—my grim reaper. I could give God the credit for my state of health; but my Episcopal

1

background did not prepare me for any spiritual under-standing of a "healing." That was what we saw on TV, with some skepticism, I might add. Here I was, though, fit as the proverbial fiddle and released to return to my law practice.

Driving along, I was trying to offer some prayers of thanksgiving to the Lord for this incredible event in my life. Even after eight months of prayer, study, and just plain living through the experience, I could not fully understand. My words were failing me, as they had each time I had prayed thanksgiving in the immediate past.

Suddenly, I began to stutter and feel somewhat con-fused. I did not realize what was happening at the moment, though I was not unfamiliar with the concept of tongues. After a few seconds of stammering, I began to pray com-fortably in a language totally unknown to me. It was scary at first, then thrilling. I continued praying in the Spirit for more than an hour. Then, I began to doubt the reality of my experience.

It is not my purpose here to comment one way or the other on the marvel of praying in the Spirit. I will just say that my encounter led me to several priests, many books on the subject, and many hours of worship in churches more Pentecostal than mine. All this authenticated the experience in my heart, and such prayer is now an integral part of my daily prayer life.

This adventure is told to set the scene for sharing with you how I have been steadily and gently led to a deeper relationship with my Lord as a direct result of having cancer. The five years since the discovery of that tumor are filled with experiences equally as exciting as that of praying in the Spirit. Today, I am engaged in various activities for the Lord that would not have occurred to me in those days.

Contrary to my hopes that afternoon, my health has not been entirely perfect. Much of that is what will be explored in this book. As of today, March 4, 1988, I am cancer–free and leading a full and wonderfully rewarding life. I do not know what the future holds, healthwise. None of us does. The one certain thing I learned from my bout with cancer is this: No one knows how long he or she is going to live. This means *no one*. It is a hard lesson to learn and an even harder one to remember. It is at the core of being able to accept God's gift of life—and to appreciate it.

Conversion, conversion to Christ, is the essence of my experience. That word could be the entire book, for it is how we are enabled to accept God's healing grace. It is a much misunderstood term. Many shy away from the entire idea. Others pridefully proclaim their conversion only to find later that they were not even close. It happens to some almost imperceptibly, over many years. To others, it can be the result of a supernatural, instantaneous, life-changing event. Paul's experience on the Damascus road (Acts 9:1-18) is proof of that.

Paul's encounter with Christ illustrates another important facet of the conversion miracle. We do not necessarily have to ask for it or even want to be converted to Christ, though we can surely resist it. Desire makes it easier, but sometimes it can happen whether we want it or not. This is not to say we cannot reject our conversion after it happens. We can, of course. There are, presumably, limits to how much Christ will do against our will.

Similarly, and equally misunderstood, we do not have to want healing, or even believe in the miracle of Christ's healing power, to be healed. We can assume the slave of the high priest who came to arrest Jesus had no faith in his Godhood. Yet, when Peter cut off his ear, Christ healed him (Luke 22:51; John 18:10).

Because these things, conversion and healing, can become a part of our lives at any time, it behooves us to learn to recognize them and, I hope, accept them and benefit from them. Things do not stop with conversion; they begin. Once we take Christ into our lives we begin to grow. This process is lifelong. A lifetime is that amount of time allotted a person by the Lord. God's perspective on time is different from ours. One day is as a thousand years.

While there is debate among some Christians on this matter, I believe that given our free will, which God so ardently protects, a person can totally reject Christ even after such a conversion experience. I will wager, though, that his or her life will never be the same.

In my case, prior to the discovery of my tumor, I was

floating along, day by day, prideful in the knowledge I was a confirmed Christian. In the forty-nine years preceding that point I had been raised in a mainline Protestant church, had had several meaningful "Spirit-filled" experiences, and had, I felt, totally accepted Christ into my heart. I am sure I had, to the degree I was able.

Beginning with my doctor's words, "You have a mass," my lines of communication to my Maker started to open, a process that continues daily. At that moment, the realization I might die loomed large before me. Risking some levity, I guess I was one of those who would casually say "*if* I die" instead of "*when* I die." I never gave it much thought.

Prayer chains were started among my church friends. My acquaintance with Jesus bloomed into a friendship. My soul was calmed and my fears allayed. There was no other explanation. Christ was at work in my heart. Do not misunderstand. The fears that remained were real. If I survived the surgery, the uncertainties of many months of convalescence still had to be met. Amidst all these problems, however, was a peace I had never known.

Was this my real conversion? I think not, not quite yet. I was not aware I was not wholly converted at that point. I learned that on April 11, 1983, the day of my surgery. The odds of my living through the operation were probably less than fifty-fifty. The night before, after several hours of various attitudes of prayer, I asked the Lord to take the cup from me, if it was his will. I had a feeling of being sacrilegious in uttering such a prayer. This was the moment of my greatest surrender to Christ in my entire life. It still is.

Nothing remarkable happened. For the remainder of the evening I visited and joked with my family and visitors. Early the next morning, after a powerful pill, I said good-bye to my mother, my sons, Steven and Charles, and my fiancée, Diana, as I was wheeled down the hall to eight hours of surgery and other procedures. I was totally unconscious until eight o'clock that night.

When I came to, my doctor was standing at the side of my bed. I slowly perceived I was in a bed with many tubes and wires attached to me. The doctor told me I was in the intensive care unit. He explained my surgery, along with some of the dangers yet to be faced. Suddenly, it hit me. I was alive! My doctor said he got all the tumor. I survived! It was at that point I knew I was healed of the cancer. It was also at that very moment that I knew I was converted. That moment remains my time of conversion. It tops all others before or since.

My life took a different direction, a different meaning, at that very moment. I am certain my real conversion required that unequivocal surrender. Never has my surrender been as total as on the eve of that surgery. I lament many times the fact it took that crisis to bring me to my knees in surrender.

2. Rule of Life

But solid food is for the mature, for those who have their faculties trained by practice to distinguish good from evil.

Heb. 5:14

I hope this account of events in my life since my first scrape with cancer will shed some light on similar problems currently being faced by many. Some things I have done of my own volition. Others I have been led into by other people. Many have been, in my opinion, gifts from God. Each happening that has affected me, from the standpoint of helping me live with cancer, deserves attention.

I hope my efforts do not come across as "preachy." If they do I can only ask the reader's indulgence. If that is the only way I can share my message with those who suffer from cancer, then so be it. If these words help one person find his or her way to living with cancer, a way that redeems that person and glorifies the Lord, the effort and attendant risk of appearing self-righteous will be worth it.

For several years prior to learning of my cancer I had done some Scripture reading and some rather random praying. The discovery of my tumor jolted me. I was filled with fear. My prognosis was poor regardless of the treatment used. Slowly, I began to feel closer to God. I started a routine of daily Bible reading and prayer. It was difficult at first. Trying to find an extra thirty minutes or so during each day is much harder than one would think. I began by making myself get up one hour earlier each day.

I had been an Episcopalian for thirty years. There had been sporadic attempts at a regular prayer life lasting various lengths of time. Somehow, each effort would lose its grip and be abandoned. I had done enough to know several effective ways to proceed. On my latest try I decided to simply use the Book of Common Prayer. Each morning I read the rite for Morning Prayer and the Scriptures appointed for that day. These consisted of an Old Testament lesson, a reading from the New Testament, and a third from one of the Gospels. The whole process took about thirty minutes.

It was hard at first. Many things and thoughts competed for that time. It was easier to nurse my anxiety over my cancer than to concentrate on the Word. Knowing many people from my church were praying for me helped me try to keep the whole situation in a spiritual perspective. Today I would say that I was feeling the effect of those prayers.

Each day I noticed a calming reaction after my Daily Office—my session with the Scriptures and the Prayer Book. It was not easy to define, only it became more discernible as the days wore on. It started my days in a mood of heeding the Lord. This influenced the rest of the day. It governed my thoughts throughout the balance of the day. More and more, some of the Bible verses spoke saliently to my unfolding plight. It reached the point, in a few weeks, where this time with God was the most important time of the day. The time arrived when I became aware of the fact that I was no longer afraid.

When I reached this point I cannot say. I perceived it more in retrospect. By the time I recognized it, it had already happened. All I could do was praise God. It was easy for me to know this strength, or absence of fear, came from the Lord. I am basically a coward, particularly when it comes to matters dealing with my tenure here on earth. The feeling of courage reached its zenith the evening prior to surgery when I surrendered totally to God. It carried me through the ensuing months of treatment and recuperation.

Once I was well, this fearlessness, or at least my awareness of it, subsided. Things were back to normal. I was back on earth. But once acquired, I found that this connection with God's Spirit was revitalized and my need for bravery met again and again.

What was I doing that plugged me into this heavenly power source? Whatever it was, I did not realize at first I was doing it. This happened prior to my total surrender to

Christ on the eve of my surgery. Of course, I had made piecemeal surrenders to the Lord on many occasions prior to that solemn night. Perhaps I was in touch and did not know it. There had been some crucial changes in my lifestyle over the years. I had been delivered from smoking and drinking and the related conduct into which those habits led me. Now I see that as deliverance by God's grace. At the time, I felt I did it by myself.

The only change in my daily habits that I can say contributed to, or caused, my feeling of peace as I approached my surgery, was my daily Bible reading and prayer sessions. Much of what I say here has been said for centuries. Perhaps hearing it in the context of my story will make it more urgent. I certainly hope so. It is so important. Without a regular (preferably daily) walk in the Scriptures and talk with God, we only handicap ourselves in any effort to cope with a life-threatening situation.

It was not until many months after I started this routine that I heard it referred to as a "rule of life." Several weeks before returning to work, a friend of mine and I spent three Spirit-filled days at Mount Calvary Retreat House, in Santa Barbara, California. This is a monastery run by the Order of the Holy Cross, an Anglican order of a Benedictine nature. The spiritual aspects of my journey through my illness came together for me during that stay. In a word, the Lord took me by the hand and showed me where I had been. It was a glorious three days.

While there I found lay people could become associates of the order. Upon exploration of this possibility with one of the good brothers, I learned a part of the requirements was to follow a rule of life. This rule required daily prayer, Scripture reading, study, and meditation. An hour each day devoted to these goals met the standard. Since I was already doing at least this much, I felt lazy as I told the brother I wanted to begin the six-month probation period to become an associate of the order.

That was easy enough, I thought. My application was accepted, and I came home from the mountaintop filled with resolve. Looking back, I offer thanks for being led to join the order. Once I was back in the saddle at the office, at home, and in life generally, trying to meet my rule of life became more and more difficult. The more I reentered the real world, the more remote and foreign my rule appeared. The thrill—yes, the thrill—of my cancer experience and its bringing me hand-in-hand with the Lord began to fade.

Alas, I had made my promise to God to live up to the Holy Cross rule of life. There were times that promise and my admiration for what God does through that holy order were the only things that got me out of bed each morning for my Daily Office, as we Episcopalians call it. It worked. After several months of following the rule, it became a habit I am not likely to break.

There are still many problems for me in this world. We will be touching on some of the major ones as this saga unfolds. Most of the time I am able to face them with a peace and calm I never had prior to my cancer experience. I attribute much of this to my rule of life.

There are, of course, many variations to the rule of life. One of the other requirements of the Holy Cross rule is taking communion every Sunday and, whenever possible, on main feast days. In denominations less liturgical this could simply mean a conscious effort at regular attendance in a Christ-centered church.

Scripture reading can be done in one of several ways or in a combination of ways. Visually we do it by reading. We can also read with our ears. There are tapes of the Scriptures that we can use at home or while driving in a car. Study can be done with tapes, audio and video, movies, television programs, and, yes, live "performances," such as sermons in church. We can plug into a rule of life for an hour a day with very little trouble. The desire is all that is required.

After some length of time (probably different for each person), we find we have developed a preference for material of a spiritual nature. As our thirst is quenched, our capacity continues to increase. We may even find ourselves switching from an enjoyable secular TV program to one of a more Christian bent. Soon it becomes clear that the world is the world is the world. Wars, famine, sickness, hate, greed, and all the other worldly traits become boring. While we are here and enmeshed in all that, a retreat to our rule of life, by whatever means, will assure us that we are not *of* those things. We are only passing through. Our rule of life is our road map.

A rule of life is but a small facet of life after conversion. It would be better to define it as the maintenance schedule for our spiritual ship. The better the care afforded our spiritual lives, the better we are able to ride the waves and storms confronting us. The more we relax and allow God to use us, the more opposition confronts us in the world. But we are not alone in our battle. God is with us. As we continue to try to grow in his way, he has his own ways of letting us know we are not alone. Many times these revelations are given us during the exercise of our rule of life. It would be a shame to be tuned into the wrong channel on the very day God was going to let us in on a miracle. The rule of life keeps us centered on him.

3. Return

And just as it is appointed for men to die once, and after that comes judgment, so Christ, having been offered once to bear the sins of many, will appear a second time, not to deal with sin but to save those who are eagerly waiting for him.

Hebrews 9:27,28

One thing proved pivotal in preparing me to accept the reality of my healing. It was an exercise in charting where I had been and where I was going. As with most of the rest of this experience, much of what I did in this regard was done unwittingly. It seemed I was gently led through the jumps by the grace of God. It was too complicated a scheme to have been planned under the stress of my illness.

After a week in intensive care and two weeks in the hospital, I was released to go home. This was in late April 1983. I left the hospital in a wheelchair. Though I was able to walk about twenty feet with the aid of a walker, I spent most of my time in bed or in a large "Lazy Boy" chair, a gift from my family to aid in my recovery. It was necessary to keep my feet up to enhance my circulation. Three or four weeks passed before I was able to walk any distance at all.

During my long hours in repose I started dictating on tape my best recollection of what had happened to me since the first visit to my doctor several months before. I had no particular aim in mind. I just wanted to preserve the facts while they were fresh in my mind. I was so weak at first I could only dictate a few minutes at a time. For reasons I did not then understand it was important to me to remember the entire episode.

Over the next six months I recorded my medical diary on a regular basis. When I finished my treatments and started back to work I had ten hours of dictation on cassettes.

I put them in a shoe box and placed them on a shelf in my closet. I had no intention to use them for any purpose save to refresh my memory, should I ever so desire.

One day, in the spring of 1984, my beloved Diana and I were going for a drive. She suggested bringing some of the tapes along so she could hear them as we motored along. As she heard the tapes she urged me to transcribe them. "There's your book," she kept saying. We both enjoyed writing, but neither had been published. "There's your book," she prodded. "There's your book."

The last thing I had in mind was taking any spare time to do the tedious "donkey work" necessary to write a book. I had done enough to know it is a very hard and thankless task. I was more interested in enjoying my new-found life by playing golf, traveling to the ocean or the mountains, and generally absorbing the "good life." Certainly, I had no desire to waste my leisure hours huddled over a typewriter.

God had different plans. He would not let me rest. If he was not spurring me on through the lovely and unrelenting pleas of Diana, he was keeping such a project stirring in my thoughts without respite. It was not long until I relented and started transcribing the tapes. Once into the mission, I became obsessed. I saw, for the first time, many of the fears and other emotions I faced during the heat of the experience. It seems I minimized the whole episode in my mind and memory—some kind of defense mechanism I guess, maybe God's mercy.

It took sixty days. Having all the data on tape simplified the work. During that time I finished the final draft of *Journey to Healing.* I had relived the pertinent aspects of my cancer experience, good and bad. The spiritual nature of my odyssey was clearer than ever. My charts and maps of my "walk with God" were now complete. Putting the book together helped me place it in true perspective. It was as though a chapter closed.

It took more than a year after the surgery for me to feel I understood the ordeal and its influence in my life. I could truly accept the fact that God had chosen to heal me. It was a wonderful realization. By placing before me the task of writing the book, God had led me gently to this truth, one I might not have been able to handle earlier. By now, I was looking at the entire episode as the most intense spiritual experience in my life. At times, as ethereal as it may seem, I was really able to give praise to God for my cancer and mean it.

About then I dusted off an old paperback book I had serendipitously rediscovered in my library. It was by a pastor in southern California, Merlin Carothers. The pithy little book he wrote and now publishes and sells is *Prison to Praise*. It is strong medicine. On prior readings I did not grasp the full meaning of its message. The essence of what Pastor Carothers says is based on Rom. 8:28: "We know that in everything God works for good with those who love him, who are called according to his purpose."

Carothers exhorts us, therefore, to praise God in everything that happens to us, no matter how bad it may seem from our point of view. The book is filled with accounts of people who have followed this path. Their lives shine in God's handiwork. I am not able to sustain such a mood for long. But when I do practice praise as described, it returns me to the frame of mind I must maintain to be at all effective for God.

Several insights that I finally perceived merit discussion. All of these matters coalesce to form the whole of my desired mind-set. One is probably no more important than another. Praise be to God, I am able to maintain this attitude most of the time. When I falter, I know I can be strengthened by prayer, Scripture reading, and, probably the quickest of all, ministering to other cancer patients and others less fortunate than I at that particular moment.

My first insight (I call it an insight; it is probably obvious to most) came as a result of a series of questions I asked myself one day driving down the highway, two years before my cancer. I was familiar with the four Gospels and had a nodding acquaintance with the rest of the Bible. Somehow, Christ's words to his disciples came to mind. This led to some flashbacks concerning who he said he was and the incidents described that would authenticate his words—things like the Transfiguration, the descending dove and voice from heaven, his miracles, and such.

I started a dialogue with myself, or whoever seemed to be talking back to me from my own brain. The question kept repeating: What if it's true? What if he is who he says he is? There was some more discussion with me. It occurred to me that what Jesus said could be very true, whether or not I chose to believe it. If it were true, there would not be much question about what we should do. We should run, not walk, to the foot of the cross and stay there to the best of our abilities. If it were not true at all, essentially we would be in the same boat as those who do not believe, though Paul would say we are to be pitied if it is false (1 Cor. 15:19).

No longer was there a choice for me. I was going to try to believe it whether I did or not. After that, it was not long until I realized I did, in fact, believe 100 percent in Jesus Christ. I had timidly opened the door to my heart just a bit. He entered. I know now that faith and the ability to believe are gifts from God. We can reject it if we choose, but faith is his gift. I let my gift lie dormant until my cancer crisis.

It must have been this gift of faith that saw me through the roughest spots of my illness. I tend to discover God's grace in retrospect. In the heat of the battle I sometimes fail to see.

A Bible passage that burned into my heart on the day I came home from the hospital is one I know I can rely on to bring me back into focus when I am assaulted by fear. I am assaulted regularly when I begin dwelling on my plight. The verse is Col. 3:3, 4: *"For you have died, and your life is hid with Christ in God. When Christ who is our life appears, then you also will appear with him in glory."*

To me, on that day, and still when I meditate on it, this meant simply that I had indeed died. I was with Christ. This world could not kill me—I had already died. From that point on I was as an alien here on earth. At some time, I know not when, my Lord will bring me home. How and when is his decision, not mine. I just have to try to be ready. It is a hard job to be ready, considering the predilection most of us have for the so-called joys of the world. It can be done, however. It can be done.

In my best moments, my moments closest to Christ, I no longer fear death. That lack of fear is fortified by bringing Christ to the dying. How simple it is, really. We are all going to die. Christians have it both ways. If they die, they win. If they live, they continue to enjoy the blessings of this life a while longer. In that regard, Christians inevitably find that, as they grow in Christ on this earth, their "worldly pleasures" become more involved with serving the Lord. Christians win either way.

The lack of fear of death equips us to live with cancer. To live for God is the reward for looking death in the eye. When the time comes to leave this earthly vale, God will usher us across the bar. Even that can be a glorious experience as exemplified by Stephen (Acts 6:15) and a multitude of martyrs throughout history. We are dead in Christ. Nothing else can kill us. Once we take our precious Lord into our hearts, we live forever. How, then, can we really be afraid to die?

Ralph Waldo Emerson said, "A hero is no braver than anyone else; he is just brave five minutes longer." We can always hold on to our faith just "five minutes longer." When we do we are returned to this earth equipped to look death full in the face and stare him down. Then we can live with cancer or anything else that may assault us.

4. The Test

In this you rejoice, though now for a little while you may have to suffer various trials.

1 Pet. 1:6

It was summer 1985. I had spent 1984 enjoying good health, finishing the manuscript of *Journey to Healing,* and going through the tedious, ten-month process of finding a publisher. On December 31, 1984, Herb Lambert, the editor of CBP Press, called to tell me they were going to publish my book. It was exciting. I took it as another sign of God's grace. With the news I was going to be a published author I became, in the eyes of some, an expert on God's gift of healing.

Here the story begins to follow its own course. I was on a roll. Things constantly fell my way. Once the book was a reality, people treated me differently; at least it seemed that way to me. In the secular world I was asked to meet with a few small groups of local writers to share my experience in writing and publishing a book. In my church, and a few others, I was asked to speak about healing and its spiritual reality.

Many sincere and otherwise knowledgeable Christians tend to view the gift of healing with suspicion. I did. In the Episcopal Church it is often lumped in with other misunderstood scriptural truths and labeled "charismatic." Many shy away from any teachings connected with any of the spiritual gifts. These people tend to explain incredible healings by attributing them to medical science, luck, or faulty diagnoses. Seldom are such events described as basic Christian life. I hope my words reach some of these brothers and sisters.

In these church meetings we explored God's wonderful

healings. I knew very little about this at that time, other than the fact I was alive. I studied, researched, and prayed. I learned about healing.

During this time, however, something was insidiously happening to me. A popular sportscaster in Texas during the fifties had a very apt phrase he used to describe a football team with a winning streak that suddenly lost the unlosable game. "They've been reading their press clippings," he would say. I guess that happened to me.

With each accolade about my upcoming book, each pat on the back after meeting with a church group, I felt more and more like a chosen person. It was hard to avoid. I was talking about something I knew very little about to people who knew even less than I. I tend to be a bit manic, sort of Walter Mittyish. I love it when I am told how smart I am or how well I do in everyday life. When this is capped by realizing that I truly did survive a massive cancer, it can be a bit staggering. This it was.

The year 1985 was thus spent basking in my glory, as it were. My glory? Only occasionally did I take time to remind myself it was not, and is not, *my* glory. The glory is entirely his, totally God's. I was so pleased he had *chosen* me as an instrument of his love and grace. I projected a lifetime in this exalted state.

Through the efforts of some of the clergy in my church, and those of my publisher, arrangements were finalized to introduce my book at the General Convention of the national Episcopal Church in Los Angeles in early September. I would be there for several days to autograph the book and help with its promotion. This was exciting. In my mind, my book was already headed for the Christian best-seller list. There was no way it could miss.

My checkups since my surgery were all clear. The months were stretching into years without a sign of a returning tumor. I felt anointed. Each passing day proved the reality of my healing. During this period two people I knew experienced cancer in their families. They called me to talk with their loved ones.

These were my first attempts at trying to minister to people with cancer. I did not find it particularly to my liking.

Once these people knew I had survived cancer, the doors were opened. I felt a deep empathy with these two people. I also watched them die. It is impossible to describe my feelings. I asked myself many times why they died and I did not. I had no answer. I had been healed; they had not. It was not up to me. My elitist frame of mind served as sufficient explanation.

The exciting parts of having one's first book published were happening. Letters arrived regularly from the editor keeping me abreast of the progress. The copies of dust-cover blurbs, advertisements, proofs of the cover, and other ego-tickling items waited in my mailbox when I came home from the office. The galley proofs of the entire book were sent to me to look over. I was now an author of national proportions. I liked the idea. How much better it would be when the book was on the market!

Reservations were confirmed in Los Angeles for the first week of the convention—the first part of September. The publisher was ahead of schedule. This was a new thrill. I knew a whole new life was opening to me. I was getting ready to welcome it with open arms. I even entertained the idea of buying a home on the California coast. That seemed a fitting place to do my writing.

During the first week of July, I had one of my routine CT scans. The doctor also wanted a complete blood work-up. After taking care of these, I went to see my doctor, Ed Felix. Our visits were always pleasant. He is a keenly intelligent man with an engaging sense of humor. Over the two years of our relationship we developed a friendship. I enjoyed our visits in spite of their subject matter.

Arriving in his office at the appointed hour, I sensed everyone seemed very busy. This was not unusual. What was different was the fact the personnel did not pass the time of day in their usual cheerful manner. It was all business. I was ushered into the examining room for my usual solitary wait for the doctor. This was generally a matter of minutes. It was the same this time. I can count on having time to notice the brands on all the medical devices, press sticks, bandages, rubber gloves and to wonder which, if any, are going to be utilized in my examination this visit.

Dr. Felix entered. Something was different. He did not have his usual little joke. He seemed absorbed the minute he entered. I wondered if some personal problem was troubling him. He was usually so affable.

"There's something on the film I don't like." That was his opening shot. I hardly had time to compute. "There's a spot on your left kidney. I'm not sure what it is. It may be nothing. We have to go in and see. If it's benign, no problem. We'll just cut it out. On the other hand, if it's malignant—we'll probably have to take the kidney."

By now, my heart was racing. I had flashbacks to that day over two years before when my other doctor said, "Here's the lump." All my fears began to well up again. I knew it. I had cancer, and I was going to die. I was not prepared for what he was telling me.

"That's just part of it," Dr. Felix continued. "I am very fearful that your right kidney was damaged beyond use in your first operation. You remember, we talked about it then."

I remembered. He had told me then that the only reason he left it in was because I had been on the operating table too long. He was reasonably sure it was damaged. "If it gives us any trouble we could go in and get it," he had explained.

I began to whine out a scenario that had me totally disabled, with no kidneys.

"I haven't even said you have cancer yet," Dr. Felix scolded. "The first thing we must do is have a kidney function test. I'll get it set up. Go have that, then we'll know where we are."

I left the doctor's office in a fog. I knew then why all the somber faces. They all knew the news was bad. I felt as though I was on a merry-go-round. It was not a new sensation.

One thing was vastly different from my first time around. Since then I had grown to know Jesus, however imperfectly. I started to pray as I drove back to the office to phone Diana and my family. Once they knew, the prayer chains were pressed into service. My peace came more quickly this time. I was able to surrender to God almost immediately. I was still scared and worried—but not like the first time.

Stretched out on the table the next day, taking the kidney test, I was both amused and saddened, realizing how foolish I had been to be so puffed up over my first healing. Here I was not even healed. Then it occurred to me that I had, indeed, been healed of that particular cancer. This was probably an entirely different one. Trying to fathom God's healing grace in the examining room of a hospital is difficult. I decided to drop it for the time.

The next day I was back in Dr. Felix's office. This time I was taken immediately to the examining cubicle. I noticed everyone in a jovial mood. At that time I did not attribute it to anything in particular. Dr. Felix entered almost immediately.

"I don't believe it," he said, beaming broadly. "Your right kidney works perfectly. That means we can proceed. I just don't believe it. I am not even sure why I left that kidney in. I would like to operate as soon as possible."

I asked if it could wait until after my autographing stint at the convention in September.

"No. Let's get it over with and be well by September." Dr. Felix does not mess around with cancer.

That is exactly what we did. The next week a carcinoma was found on my left kidney. They took the kidney. While in there, a Duke's tumor was found on a portion of my colon. About two feet of colon was removed. I was hooked back up and eventually sent on my way.

The terminology of cancer is ominous. As explained to me, carcinoma is a malignant and invasive tumor. The other names we hear simply tell the doctors where and what the tumor is. The only terms that mattered to me were malignant and benign. Malignant means the tumor is life-threatening. I never heard the term benign used to describe any of my tumors. The term "Duke's tumor" meant simply a malignancy in the colon. It was popular because that was the way the press described the tumor causing the removal of part of President Reagan's colon within a few days of my similar operation.

There was a kind of ho-hum feeling on my part during the month I devoted to this second operation. I was in the hospital seven days. Everything went without a hitch. There were no problems. This was so different from the first massive surgery, with the intensive care ward and long recuperation period. From the time I entered the hospital I was somehow able to effectively place myself in God's hands. The peace, lack of fear, and even lack of pain were evident throughout this experience.

Felix was not alarmed about either cancer. They were detected early and, in the case of the colon, a healthy margin of good tissue surrounding the tumor was removed. The good news was that I would not be taking any radiation or chemotherapy. Calling this entire episode routine may sound like an understatement. I feel the grace of God enabled me to treat it in such a light. When I dwell on where I have been, I know it is not routine. That is, I think, a part of his healing. He gives us a hindsight that places things more nearly in his perspective.

There are times I feel as though I am experiencing what war veterans describe as "delayed-stress syndrome." A "free-floating anxiety" starts to engulf me. This is not often, maybe once or twice a year. Of course, before all the cancer, I felt anxious on occasions. This is not like that. This, I think, is directly attributable to a subconscious realization of the gravity of my illnesses.

When these spells begin, I remind myself that I am well, for now, and functioning at full speed. I now have more moments walking with God than ever before. This must be at least a part of his wonderful gift of being healed. Then I remember when I was first reminded, by one of the good brothers at Mount Calvary, that "even Lazarus died." My fears dissolve and I praise God.

I made the convention in good health. It gave me ample time to begin to rethink my position on healing. In this respect I had been deflated. I had to start over again, this time not as the expert but as the man who now had known four different kinds of cancer (including skin cancer) in a little over two years. The positive side, I knew, was that I was still here and functioning normally. Praise God.

5. Growth

Like newborn babes, long for the pure spiritual milk, that by it you may grow up to salvation; for you have tasted the kindness of the Lord.
1 Pet. 2:2, 3

The drive from the convention site (just across from Disneyland), up through the San Gabriel Mountains, across the Mojave Desert toward Texas, could not have been more inspiring that wonderful September morn. After three days at the 1985 General Convention of the national Episcopal Church I was filled with new ideas and insights. I was taking my vacation and doing something I had not done before. I was taking an extended auto trip, through New Mexico and Texas, some 3500 miles, all by myself. Diana, my fiancée, was unable to get away for any of these two weeks. This was disappointing to both of us. But, we kidded, they would not postpone the convention.

Until this trip I was, normally, a social creature. I did not enjoy being alone for long periods of time. But this trip gave me the opportunity to do a lot of sorting out, some distilling of my thoughts. The convention proved to be successful from the standpoint of book sales. I was introduced to a phenomenon that would shape my activities then and in time to come.

Now that there was an actual book to see, hold, and talk about, the doors opened for me to discuss my disease and my present state of health almost at every turn. I talked with people from all sectors: priests, bishops, doctors and lay men and women from all over the country. After three days at the General Convention, it had become very natural for me to speak about my experience. The supernatural, special-chosen aspects of my feelings about what was happening were no longer there. Now it was simple. I had had cancer.

Now I was cancer-free. In a spiritual sense I identified with the blind man Christ healed. I was blind. Now I see.

The convention was an eye-opener. Spiritually, I found myself a bit overwhelmed at the power and wealth represented by that gathering of Anglicans. I engaged in many in-depth conversations with the deputies and visitors. Each encounter cemented my faith in Christ's Church. My knowledge of healing, and more importantly, healings, was widened. Healings are indeed miracles. The wonderful discovery was that they are not rare. Miracles happen all the time. We are not always open to noticing them.

At other times I had to smile inwardly at all the scurry and hustle and bustle. Watching the delegates, particularly the bishops, hurrying to and from their appointed meetings, in their purple shirts and backward collars, was quite a sight. With all the color, medallions, and other regalia, I felt that I was in the Vatican. There were also times, I must admit, when I felt I was with Alice in Wonderland or Dorothy in the Land of Oz.

Driving east into the morning sun, I reflected on this wonderful experience in my life. I felt a closeness with my Maker. I gave thanks to him for being alive and able to be a part of it all. My surgery was less than two months old. Occasionally, my scar would remind me of this reality if I stayed too long in one position. The only effect I noticed at the convention was that I tired more easily than usual. I was up and around all day, each day. At the end of these sessions I would be exhausted. Each day, however, I grew stronger.

Because I was going to be traveling alone, I dusted off my old CB radio. Years before I had become proficient in the art of "modulatin' " with the "18-wheelers." Now, my fluency in the argot suffered from a lack of practice.

After leaving Needles, California, I was making that long, gentle climb up toward Kingman, Arizona, and on to Flagstaff. The road goes from near sea level to 7,000 feet in that stretch. My CB was on. Not much out of the ordinary was happening. I love to drive. I was just cruising along, enjoying my elated mood and feeling blessed to be alive and in God's care.

"Breaker, breaker," squawked the CB. "Anybody out there got a copy?" From his accent, this guy could have been from my old hometown of Sweetwater, Texas. He sounded like Gunsmoke's famous Chester. I reached for my mike to respond. I was too late.

"Go ahead, breaker," came a deep voice from a man who could have grown up next door to us both.

"Let's take it down to 12. I want to jaw awhile," requested the first. CB protocol requires switching to a free frequency when a long conversation is going to take place. This leaves the designated "truckers' " channel open for the use of the drivers in relaying road conditions, weather reports, and, most important of all, the ubiquitous "smokey reports." These keep anyone with a CB on advised of the location of the stalwart members of the highway patrols. It is seldom realized that it likewise keeps the patrol members aware of the locations of the broadcasters.

Rank curiosity led me to tune down to channel 12 with these two gentlemen. Normally, when one does that, the reward is a rather folksy conversation concerning the family, the kids, the bowling team, and the last cookout staged at the home of one of the participants. On this fine day I was privy to two of the most astounding witnesses to Christ's miraculous power I have heard on CB, or anywhere. I must have been traveling along in the same direction as these men, as I was able to listen to their colloquy for twenty or thirty minutes.

One told of his powerlessness over alcohol until his marriage to a "church" woman. He detailed how she had, through love, gotten him off the booze and into a church. He was now active and praising God over the airways. The other, with great emotion, was led to tell of his coming to the Lord and how it saved his marriage to a wonderful woman. I could not believe it. Was God telling me something? I could not contain myself.

"Breaker, one, two. Breaker, one, two," I said into my mike.

"Go ahead, breaker," came the answer.

"Is this a private session, or can anyone witness to our Lord?" I asked.

"Anybody," one of them laughed. "Come back."

I gave my story. I told them of my cancer—now my cancers. I spoke of God's healing grace and the profound blessing my cancer turned out to be. They understood when I said it was a blessing because it was where I met Jesus. We "modulated" about the love of our Lord and his miracles for several minutes. Then, as one of them was responding to my witness, the signal left my set, and I never heard anymore. I was sorry I could not thank them for including me in their mobile group session. I wondered who they were.

Time was going by rapidly. I was quite touched by my encounter with the truck drivers. It touches me today as I tell about it. I felt God was not going to let up on me until I had no doubts as to his reality and his miracles. It was working.

I was making such good time I decided to pass on through Flagstaff and bed down at Winslow, Arizona. In the last hour or so of my drive that day, I turned off the radios and the tape player and simply meditated on all that had happened to me over the past few days. I should do that more often. It is important just to be alone with one's thoughts and one's God. It helps things fall into place for me. I learned this lesson well on this trip. I had plenty of time. During some of those hours I found I did not want any television, any radio, any company, or even any reading save for a few verses from the Scriptures. It took me many years to discover this.

Arriving at Winslow just after dark, I checked into a motel. I decided to treat myself to a good steak, one of the occasional indulgences I allow myself. The evening was spent watching people in the cafe, watching the evening news on TV, and falling unretrievably asleep in the glow of the tube. I slept soundly. I was a very thankful man.

6. Home

Go home to your friends, and tell them how much the Lord has done for you, and how he has had mercy on you.

Mark 5:19b

My big chair on the sun porch was still there. Since my first visit to Mount Calvary Retreat House in 1983, this was my favorite spot in the monastery. It was large enough for my frame and was situated so I had a wonderful view of the town of Santa Barbara, the mountains behind it, and the Pacific Ocean. The luxury afforded me in this position almost precluded any serious study or reading. Because most of the other guests would join me on the porch at one time or another, it was a great place to meet people and become involved in the therapeutic discussions that inevitably enriched my retreats.

The weather was heavenly this late September afternoon in 1985. I had arrived at Mount Calvary earlier in the day. This was to be the final four days of my vacation. I was ready. Sitting on the porch, drinking in the magical view, I was lazily reviewing my trip to Texas. There were not many guests yet, so I had this afternoon to myself for reflection and rest. I drove from Texas in just over two days, and I was road-weary.

The woman who acts as secretary and general office manager to the order, Georgeanne, was working in her office. Her desk was directly off the porch so it was easy to visit with her if time allowed. After some pleasant conversation about my survival for over two years and the good news about my book, she went back to work and I resumed my reverie. I noticed one other person. There was a nice-looking, well-dressed man sitting in the library with the doors closed. This room also was next to the porch at the other end. Through the glass doors I could see he was deeply involved with his work.

On my way to claim my turf—the chair—I strolled through the little hallway that serves as the bookstore. I mainly wanted to see if the brother in charge had stocked any copies of my recently released book. He had. There were five in a stack on one of the shelves. Now it is not such a big deal. Then it was quite a thrill. I leaned back in my chair and thought how nice it would be if I autographed all those books.

Between catnaps I reviewed my trip, from the convention to Santa Barbara. I had taken ten days to visit with friends and relatives in Albuquerque, New Mexico; Odessa, Texas and its environs; and El Paso. I had visited bookstores and introduced my book. I had sold or given away the entire box of fifty books I had taken to the convention in case they were needed. The visits with my friends were fun. I had regaled them with the vagaries of getting a book published, as if I were an old pro.

In 1983, after the discovery of my first cancer, my mother and I made much this same tour. Diana flew to meet us in Texas. Mother and I drove back to California over the same roads I had just traversed. It felt a little eerie. In 1983 I had been given little hope of seeing this country again. On that trip I nursed intermittent forebodings that I was on my last trip to Texas. Here I was in 1985, more than the predicted two years later, retracing the steps of my earlier swan song. It felt good. I savored the feeling that afternoon in the huge chair overlooking the blue Pacific.

I was healed. I was still here. It was in this same chair that I had read the Book of Job on my first stay at Mount Calvary. That was during my recuperation after my first surgery. It helped to learn about Job. On this trip I reread Job. He still spoke to me. Oddly, my second bout with cancer did not make me doubt the healing of my first. The second episode only deepened my belief in God's healing powers.

Over the next days my illness, my health, and my book were the topics of many conversations with the brothers and the other guests. My books were all sold from the shelf of the bookstore. Autographs were requested. It was a new feeling for me, and I grew to like it.

Through all this the man in the library continued his work. He was not staying at the retreat house. He arrived around ten in the morning, worked all day, and left late in the afternoon. He did share the noon meal with us, but without much conversation.

After lunch on the last afternoon of my stay, several of us gathered on the porch. We were discussing God's miracles in general and healing in particular. The man in the library had moved his books and materials to a table at the far end of the porch. He worked along as we talked. We learned earlier that he was a minister. We never knew in which denomination.

About an hour into the conversation someone asked the minister if he would like to join in the discussion. He declined politely, explaining that in his opinion, the gifts and miracles we were discussing, including healing, just did not happen today.

"Did you hear," someone asked, "this gentleman right here has been healed of cancer?"

"Yes, I overheard," replied the minister. "There are other logical explanations besides a miraculous healing. God used those at the beginning of the Church to prove who Jesus and his disciples were. He doesn't need to do that now."

"Have you read Ken's book?"

"No, I haven't. I heard you all discussing it. I have some time. I'll be happy to look at it. I read pretty fast."

"That's fair enough," said one of the guests.

I was just sitting by, watching it all unfold. The guest handed the preacher his copy of the book. He took it and retired to the library, shutting the door behind him.

The rest of us continued our discussions for the rest of the afternoon. Some would leave for a spell to take a walk outside or visit with some of the other guests. It so happened most of the original participants in the healing discussions were there on the porch when, an hour and a half later, the minister emerged and returned the book to its owner.

"What did you think?" asked the lender of the book.

"Very interesting," replied the minister, pensively. "I only have one thing to say about it. If God heals, he only does it for his glory, not ours."

We all smiled. "We couldn't agree more, pastor," one of the other guests said. "We couldn't agree more."

With that, the bells rang announcing the Vesper service in the chapel. The minister told us all good-bye, saying he had finished his work. We all gave him a good hug and wished him Godspeed. He packed up and left. We all went into the chapel. A solid community had been established during the afternoon.

I left Mount Calvary before breakfast the next morning. I was filled with God's Spirit. I had been wonderfully recharged by my stay. It was always that way. The atmosphere and the community formed by the other guests and the brothers combine to ensure one's spiritual refueling.

The response people had to my book was pleasing. I was getting a hint at how my book opened doors for me to share and witness about Christ. I felt I was some kind of medical curiosity, though this was lessening. It was not a bad feeling. Mainly, it was a sensation of being very glad to be alive.

The fact I had just had surgery for further cancer did not diminish others' enthusiasm about the divine intervention happening in my life. I had thought it would. This helped me return, over and over, to the lesson I learned the first time. God's greatest healing is a healing of the spirit. He may allow a limb to grow back as some have reported; he may let the deaf hear or the blind see; he may remove tumors and heal cancers; but the quintessential healing is the healing of the spirit.

Another way to view this is from the standpoint of someone who is dying. This person is not going to be, for whatever reason, restored to health in this world. It has been said that the ultimate healing from God is to be taken home to be with him. I believe this. Christians profess this. Knowing this is extremely comforting when one loses a loved one. Knowing the deceased had accepted Christ assures us the ultimate healing has transpired.

The ultimate healing cannot, however, be accomplished

without knowing and accepting Christ for who he says he is—the Son of God. This must be done in this lifetime. When one suddenly falls deathly ill there may not be time. If that person is inexplicably healed it should be the beginning of the healing of the spirit. Certainly, one can deny God at any time. We have free will. But when God works to heal the spirit, that denial becomes almost impossible.

A healing that heals the spirit may not heal the physical impairments. A person so healed will still shine for God. God's strength is in our weakness, Paul explains. The spirit may be healed minutes before death. The point is, if the spirit is healed, death is the ultimate healing. Without a healed spirit, the ultimate healing is not attained.

These were just some of the thoughts rolling around in my mind as I headed north toward Fresno. These were the things we retreatants had discussed, debated, and tried to resolve. For some it was an introduction to the concept of God's healing. For others, it was just an interesting exercise. For me, it helped to distill the thoughts, feelings, and hazy insights I experienced because of my second surgery.

Most of what I was learning I had learned the first time around. I saw now how I let it slip away. I left the monastery with two lessons in my heart. One was, again, the concept of the healing of the spirit superceding even the healing of the body. The other was the concept of urgency—the fact we do not know when our last chance to take Christ into our lives will be. It could easily be today.

Five hours later I arrived home. It did not take me long to enjoy dinner with my beloved Diana. We loved to share each other's thoughts on what was happening in our spiritual lives. I had plenty to share after this trip. I was thankful I had a companion of Diana's spirituality with whom to share it. Not many would understand, I feared. Not many would understand.

7. Stigma

For my yoke is easy, and my burden is light.

Matt. 11:30

My life settled into its own groove after returning from my Texas trip. Those weeks after my second surgery helped me regain my humanity. Since my first bout with cancer, now almost three years before, my concept of God's healing grace had broadened. The magic was no longer present when I talked about or thought about miracles. I learned miracles are a way of life.

Some would argue that these thoughts dealt with the supernatural. They grumbled that my religion was one that believed in magic. My answer to them was simple. Of course, Christianity is a religion based on the supernatural. What could be more supernatural than the resurrection? That is the basis of our beliefs.

Magic, in the sense of being sorcery, it is not. Supernatural it is, in the sense that God is a power greater than humankind, who revealed himself through his Son, Jesus, and who is able to cause miracles. God heals. I know that. He healed me of cancer twice. He continues to heal me, thereby allowing my spirit to grow more and more healthy as I remain on this earth.

My knowledge of this healing and my ultimate acceptance of that gift from my Lord do not, however, assure me of a life without problems. As I got back into my law practice the second time around, I was reminded of some of the concerns I recognized after my first surgery. The elated mood created by knowing I had been healed, the writing and publishing of the book, and the attention paid to me when I spoke concerning my healing, all continued to insulate me from some of the stark realities cancer brings into one's life.

Now, I was back to earth. Now I could discern the look of surprise on the face of one I had not seen for awhile. Some even said such things as "I heard you had died" or "Oh, you're back to work," 18 months after the fact.

One day in early 1986, when I had been back in the office several months after the kidney removal, my partner, Truman, came into my office. He explained that one of our clients wanted to take his file and go to another law office. I was the attorney working on his case.

"He said he is happy with the way you're handling the matter. It's just that he needs a lawyer he knows will make it to court when the time comes."

My partner was very upset with this client.

"I told him you'll be there, that you are cancer free now," he said. "He just said that he knows with cancer it is just a matter of time and his case is too important."

Of course, I was hurt. I was disappointed the client did not come directly to me. I had put many hours in on his problem, after both the first operation and the second.

Truman continued, "He would not understand. I didn't realize there was that much prejudice against someone who has had cancer. I had no choice. I gave him his file. I'm sorry, Ken. I didn't know what else to say."

After Truman left I could suddenly remember many instances of condescending treatment at the hands of some people. Some were mere acquaintances; others were friends. Even prior to my second trip to the hospital, I noticed many of my clients were not returning. I remembered when I had treated people with cancer in the same way.

Prior to my illness, I knew cancer was a death sentence. My experience in my own family proved that to me. My father and my two sisters died from cancer. Once it was discovered, it was just a matter of time. I saw now that the general public held the same misconception.

Once I learned of my cancer I tried to find out as much as I could about it. It is fair to say that 50 percent of the people diagnosed as having cancer today will be cured. One doctor wrote that there are some 260 different kinds of cancer; each one has been cured at least once. If discovered in time, much can be done to effect a cure. My latest surgery was proof of that. We found it early, we got it, and statistically, I was told, that should be it.

That is a positive side of cancer, today. While it is a deadly disease, it is only one of many deadly diseases. I remember a time with my first cancer when I felt relieved to be advised, mistakenly, I had another condition, not cancer. The other condition was just as fatal, being a serious condition of the pancreas. But I actually felt comfort in learning I was not going to die of cancer. As it turned out, of course, I did have cancer. I laugh at myself now when I remember that episode. I could have died from the other condition more contentedly than from cancer. Cancer does strange things with our heads.

I could not go on a one-man crusade to educate the public about cancer. That was being done by several organizations. I could only live out my life as God gave it to me. Now he was leading me into several new ministries. The main one was still talking to groups about the healing experience.

Slowly, I became increasingly involved in visiting people with cancer. As my book's circulation increased, opportunities to visit cancer patients grew. One thing became clear. If I was involved with another person who was going through what I had been through, I did not have the time or the inclination to dwell on the acts of prejudice aimed against me, and there were several on a fairly regular basis.

It is not healthy to dwell on this stigma. I mention it here to alert the reader to its existence. It is subtle. It can be depressing. In some cases it can create huge problems, as when a person, otherwise capable, is denied employment. Many doors are probably closed once it is learned there is cancer in the medical history. People think if a person has cancer, cured or not, he or she is not going to live out a natural life span.

I have said it before, but it bears repeating. The one very clear lesson I learned from my cancer is this: No one knows how long he or she is going to live. The more I know this fundamental truth, the greater sense of urgency I feel to bring my friends and loved ones to the Lord. Ideally, that fact would neutralize the stigma and prejudice connected with cancer. In many circles it does not.

To end this part of the discussion with a touch of irony I want to tell the rest of the story of the man who came and got his file—the one who was afraid I might not live long enough to take care of him. His case came up for trial about eight months after he took it to another lawyer. On the day before his hearing in court, my former client died suddenly from a heart attack. I use this sad fact many times to illustrate the uncertainty of our walk on this earth, with or without cancer.

By the grace of God I learned to handle with good humor the diffidence with which I am treated by some people. The fact that I have learned to live with my rather terrifying medical history does not mean that others have. Cancer will always be a very scary and misunderstood disease, at least until a sure and easy cure is found. I think we are close. This is what keeps me following the doctor's orders. I want to outlive it, if I can. There are other ways I would prefer leaving this good earth.

God began to lead me gently into situations that did not allow me time to worry. Diana was great about helping me keep my spirits high. She had known great tragedy in her life. She looked to her God and to the beautiful things in life, such as music and art, to keep her mind focused on the Lord and his will. During 1986 we both spent many hours dealing with cancer patients and others less fortunate than we. We always knew we received more blessing than we gave.

There were moments of self-pity on my part, of course. Many times I almost had to be dragged to visit and pray with a person whose cancer was overwhelming. But when I did, my "pity party" was over. This self-pity, I saw, was more like grief. We grieve for a friend with cancer. I was grieving for one of my closest friends—me.

Upon reflection, I realized how fortunate I was to have such a normal, healthy life. I was not disabled in any way unless I let my fears overcome me. When I remembered the first insights I had—that I had died and was with Christ, that I was just passing through, and, most importantly, that my spirit was healed—I could carry on feeling strong.

Sometimes I even recalled a little joke that helped me put my thoughts in perspective. On one of my desk calendars I found a little quip attributed to Woody Allen, the gifted humorist. I cut it out and placed it under the glass top of my desk. It helped me maintain my sense of humor, a terribly important weapon. Woody says, sardonically, "It's not that I am afraid of dying. I just don't want to be there when it happens." A bit irreverent perhaps, but a very thought-provoking observation.

As our spirits are healed, a life-long process, we become more and more equipped to "be there when it happens." Praise God!

8. Normalcy

Put in your sickle, and reap, for the hour to reap has come, for the harvest of the earth is fully ripe.

Rev. 14:15b

A time came when cancer, particularly mine, was not the predominant thing on my mind. It took many months, even years. With the rarity of my first cancer and the odds against a person's having and surviving multiple primary cancers, as was my case, it was easy for me to keep it in the forefront of my thoughts.

This point of being able to go long periods of time without giving my cancer a thought was reached shortly before the second operation, in 1985. Perhaps the writing of the book and going through the required replays prolonged the period. No matter, the second siege shattered my ability to treat the disease with any degree of objectivity. I thought, at times, I must be boring everybody to death with my war stories about cancer. I consciously tried not to discuss it.

In the summer of 1986 I suddenly realized I was no longer obsessed with the fact I was the victim of such a rapacious illness. Without knowing where or when I slipped across the line, I was able with God's help to keep my underlying fears at bay. People had to show a sincere interest before I would go into any detail concerning my health. I don't think I was being falsely modest. It was just no longer the total object of my thoughts. As with anything else, with all but the very closest of family and friends, once one is on his feet, his illness is "last week's news."

When I became fully aware of this state of mind, I was pleased. I did not attach any particular significance to it. There was no cosmic message. I did try to figure out how it happened, however. Cancer can take over an individual.

Beyond that, cancer can take over an entire family with its legacy of gripping fear. I have seen times when the patient defeated this fear, but his loved ones did not.

This brings me easily to a discussion of those factors I feel helped me reach this point of détente with my devil, cancer. It was an armed truce. I continued to see my doctor and have my checkups religiously. My vantage point was now very different. Up to this point, a year or so after my second surgery, I always had the feeling that cancer was coming after me. Now, oddly, I felt that we had cancer on the run. "We" was made up of God and me. God was seeing to it I had the finest medical care, and I was trying to cooperate in every way I could.

With my mind cleared to the degree that it was, I found that I turned my time and energies outward. I started to write more. I was spending much of my nonoffice time writing. I was enjoying it.

My hours spent playing the banjo in a Dixieland band were still a large part of my life. Music is very important and, as many have pointed out, very therapeutic.

Through my deepening friendship with the vicar of our little mission, John Rollinson, I was being slowly led into a deeper understanding of the truths I had been discovering viscerally in my responses to my illnesses. I had unearthed nothing new and novel. I was just being blessed by having the opportunity to see these godly forces at play in my life. My spiritual companion and director, the Reverend John Rollinson, was feeding me the elementary profundities of Christian orthodoxy as fast as I could take them. I found I soaked them up like a sponge.

The Lord was again leading me by the hand. If something happened in the course of a visitation to a sick person, I could discuss it with John. He is not afraid to accept as reality the miracles of God's action and God's interplay in our lives. I learned God is intimately involved in the minute, even boring, facets of our daily walks. The more I allowed myself to grow spiritually, the more I could see God's handiwork. It was absolutely thrilling.

We reach the point where we have to laugh at the obvious manner in which God places in our paths opportunities to serve him. I have been known to miss some and trip over others. I have also been known to recognize some and act on them. What a wonderful feeling that is! Sometimes our Lord may even give us an "atta boy" or an "atta girl." If not, our hearts will tell us we were God's utensils that day. Praise God.

We must, I found, be readily available. Our function is to help him take the gospel to all the world. For some, the mission field may be Africa. Ours may be the house next door or the person with whom we are doing business that day. Even our best friend who somehow does not quite understand our growing involvement in matters Christian might be the one. We never know. We may be of life-changing help to someone, bringing him or her to Christ, and never know it. We do not have to know. We simply must strive to be accessible to God for his use.

A story I heard illustrates what I am trying to say. A prominent minister from my town flew into San Francisco early one morning to attend a meeting. It was his hope to be back home that same evening. His schedule had been back-breaking for several weeks. In the evening, when he boarded the plane for home, he was relishing the idea that he would get an hour's sleep on the flight to Fresno. The seat next to him was even empty.

He fell asleep before the plane took off from San Francisco. At the very last minute a passenger boarded and took the seat next to the preacher. He awoke momentarily. He thought to himself he should probably introduce himself and maybe see if there was an opportunity to introduce his traveling friend to Jesus. Instead, the good preacher went back to sleep and stayed there until he arrived in Fresno.

This minister relates a little conversation he had with his Lord as he was driving home from the airport. In effect, the Lord scolded him for not following his first impulse to evangelize his seatmate. "You cannot imagine the flights I had to change and the reservations I had to cancel just to get that man in that seat next to you for that hour," said God to our friend. He knew then he had dropped the ball. He blew it.

That story was told me as true. I think of it often. We

have to try not to drop the ball. We have to try not to blow it. This kind of life can be intense. There are times when we have to withdraw and take a few deep breaths. Sometimes I have to delay getting involved with another cancer patient. I am not much good to the patient or the family if I am exhausted. Prayer and openness to God's promptings are all we need to know when we are ready. He lets us know. It is not mysterious. At times his leadings are clearer than the proverbial noses on our faces.

Throughout 1986 I made every effort to discern and follow the Lord's directions in my life. It was very exciting. For the most part I found that my book had opened doors for me to visit cancer patients. One led to another. My ministry at that time was more one of visitation than anything else. When I was on my back with cancer I found a visit from someone who had lived through it quite uplifting.

I was still shy about offering to pray for the person I was visiting. If he or she or a member of the family requested it, I would pray. Once in a great while I would lay hands on the person and pray for healing. I only did this when asked or if I knew the person well and knew he or she was an understanding Christian. This was not the case too many times, I am sad to say.

During that year I was involved with about a dozen such people. There were several visits to the hospitals for each one. Sometimes the relationship would develop to where I would visit in the home, if the person went home. In each case, the cancer was discovered late, the person's general health was not good, or he or she would not follow the instructions of the doctors concerning a course of treatment. Most of these people died before long.

After a few episodes I thought I recognized a phenomenon. I called it a death wish. I discussed this with the family members and the doctors and found it is a very real component of a disease such as cancer. For reasons only the patient can tell, the drive or will to fight back is not there. It is probably a combination of fear and possibly an underlying unhappiness to begin with. I know this was the case in one of the people with whom I spent much time during his last month.

All doctors having anything to do with my first surgery, the big one, told me they could only do 50 percent of it. The rest was up to me. I know now my attitude and will to survive were and are gifts from God. I long to know how I can impart this to some of those I visit. I cannot. Perhaps, though, the Lord can use me as a reminder that such gifts are real.

Rather than finding these visitations depressing, I found each one to be a blessing to me. Most of the time I could not see where I was doing anything but making someone's last days a little less dull. I had never done any significant visitation of the sick before. I remembered what I felt like when I was being visited in the hospital. I laugh now. Three or four people would come into my room, say hello to me with very long faces, and then turn to each other for a long visit or to share a TV program. After the first greeting, I was like the furniture.

Asking me questions that required me to spend any energy thinking was a source of some resentment on my part. As I began to feel better this was not too bad. Remembering my feelings helped me tailor my approach on my visits to the cancer patients. When a person gets well enough to enjoy company in the hospital, he or she will probably be discharged.

By fall 1986, I had my life well under control, I thought. I was busier than I had ever been prior to my cancer. I surely thought I was working for the Lord in the area he desired. I was doing more evangelizing accidentally than I had done in my whole life on purpose. I was enjoying it. I was beginning, in a sense, to read my press clippings again.

One night I was working on a little article for a local paper. I had the television going in the background. Most of the time I can write with it on—if the program doesn't require too much attention or thought. I will leave it to the reader to decide how much interference most programs cause.

On this particular night the program was one of the religious broadcasts I was watching more and more. I think it was the 700 Club, though I could not say for certain. Several times during the course of the program I overheard them talking about some kind of invasion—an invasion into some prison somewhere, I thought. I kept writing and did not pay it much mind.

Again, the announcement came about the prisons. It was beginning to pique my interest. Several years of my legal practice were devoted to the practice of criminal law. I was not unfamiliar with the inside of jails and prisons. The next time they began to talk about this so-called invasion, I started to pay attention.

During the next ten minutes I learned of a prison ministry. I found that many people go into the prisons of this country to try to bring the reality of Jesus Christ to the men and women confined there. I heard two short witnesses by ex-convicts about their conversions to Christ because of this type of ministry. A national invasion was being planned where thousands of Christian volunteers would go into the prisons, all over the nation, on the same day. That day was coming in a few weeks.

Back to my typing. That was interesting. I thought how great it was that people would take time to do that. I was sure it was a very thankless task. There was nothing nice about any prison I had ever seen, and I had seen a few. "I've put all the time I want inside the walls of some jailhouse or prison," I thought, as I continued to write.

The last announcement on this program was Chaplain Ray, of Dallas, Texas, trying to recruit people to become involved in the prison invasion. I said, "Good luck," and dismissed it. At the very last minute a telephone number was flashed across the bottom of the screen. We were being asked to call this toll-free number for further information. To this day I do not know what made me pick up the phone. I dialed. I hoped the number was going to be busy. It was not. I heard myself telling the pleasant voice on the other end of the line that I would like to receive the information. Three days later, I did.

Where this led is the subject of a later chapter. Suffice it to say here that I was put in touch with the head pastor of the local prison ministry. I was too late for the prison invasion because I had missed the training session. But they sure wanted me to consider joining them in the local jail ministry—that is, if I checked out securitywise. This was my inauspicious introduction to another ministry that has since filled my heart with blessings.

These two ministries, cancer patients and prisoners, are two of the most important things the Lord has given me. They are "bottom-line" ministries. There is little time for frills. These people are hungry for the gospel. At first, I thought I was taking advantage of a cancer patient when I would try to evangelize. Now I know, that may be the first time in that person's life when he or she is receptive to the Word. It is the same with prisoners. These are the front lines.

In my opinion, these two ministries and my being blessed enough to be involved with them account for my state of mind, and thus my state of general good health, today. Getting me into these ministries must be another part of God's plan for my healing. Certainly, such ministries are continual sources of healing to my spirit. They help keep my spirit healthy. God can heal our bodies and our spirits. We have an obligation to do all we can to keep them healed.

There is not much time left in my daily rounds to dwell on some obvious questions that, of course, rattle around in the back of my mind. They can all be summed up with two questions. What's next? Who knows? When such questions crop up I remind myself I have gotten this far, with God's help. I know that with God's help I will get wherever he wants me to be. If I try to do it by myself, I go backwards. I really try earnestly to do whatever it takes to keep plugged into God's will for me. As time goes by it seems to be easier and easier. Praise the Lord!

9. The Vineyard

I was sick and you visited me, I was in prison, and you came to me.
Matt. 25:36b

In March 1987 several of us were on our way to a large, maximum security prison in a small town 130 miles from Fresno. This morning's group consisted of ten men and women. We gathered at the home of one of the couples at six in the morning, had some prayer and coffee, and hit the road. We were to be in the prison chapel, ready to go, at ten. We were riding in a large van provided by one of the members for this purpose.

By now, I had been out to the road camp, or branch jail, as it was called, several times. Our group took a bare-bones church service to that institution two Sundays each month. At this point I was hooked on the prison ministry. There is something quite touching about a group of prisoners at worship in a sparsely appointed room set aside as a little church.

At road camp most of the men and women are serving time for less serious crimes. In the prisons, some are serving sentences of twenty to thirty years or more, some for very serious offenses. At road camp the crimes are less ugly. Most of the prisoners are serving less than a year for matters generally related to drugs or alcohol. Petty thievery, bogus checks, petty theft—crimes like that took them there. Once in a while one will see a seasoned criminal at road camp. He will be on his way to or returning from a prison.

The contrast presented by these men in our little church service and those in the big recreation room next door is great. Most of the men and women in church are serious about what is being presented. It is hard to be a Christian in a jail or prison. Peer pressure is the force that rules.

Making a statement for Christ in this atmosphere is a brave act. Only about 10 percent of the prison population is able to do so in a lasting manner. In those who do, statistics are showing the rate of recidivism is 5 to 10 percent, as opposed to 60 to 80 percent in those who do not. Some wardens report less tension in a prison where there is an active group of Christians.

"This is your first time going into a big prison, isn't it, Ken?" The woman asking this question was Margie. She and her friend Shirley were the two on this trip I knew best from our trips to the jail.

Margie is a delightful and refreshing woman of Mexican heritage who has an uncanny ability to relate to the men in the prisons and jails. Her Christian commitment is deep and real. Even though her life has not been easy, she adds a note of fun and enjoyment to our trips to the prisons.

Shirley is likewise Hispanic. The Hispanic population inside the walls of these institutions is large. Many do not speak English. We, therefore, must be equipped to minister to them in their language. Shirley is a saintly woman. Her talks to the men speak right to their spirits. Her chief ministry outside the prison is to street people. She ministers to them on a one-on-one basis, starting her dialogue many times by offering a sandwich from her purse.

All of the members of the prison ministry are deeply committed. There are too many to mention here. The leader of our group, Eddie Ronquillo, is a former prisoner who found Christ in prison. He, and his lovely wife, Evangelina, have earned national acclaim for their work in establishing the prison ministry in central California.

"Yes, Margie, this is the first," I answered somewhat absentmindedly. I was riding along, looking out the window, just doing a little idle musing. Margie's question pulled my mind back inside the vehicle. I had been looking at the familiar landscape and lazily giving thanks to God for my life. In the three months prior to this event I had met a group of "bed-rock" Christians, as I called them. These men and women were from various church traditions—Pentecostal, Evangelical, Roman Catholic, and, yes, now even Episcopal. I did have trouble sometimes trying to explain just what an Episcopalian is to some of my new friends.

For three months I watched these people donate hours of their lives to bring the reality of Christ to the prisons. Each time I participated in a service I was amazed that I left feeling so blessed. I would go trying to bring a blessing to these prisoners; I would leave with my heart filled with God's blessing. It never failed.

These people who visit the prisons allow their Christianity to rule every moment of their lives. They live, breathe, and eat with Jesus Christ. Their work inside the prisons is selfless. I was overwhelmed. I certainly do not want to trivialize my description of the depth of faith these people have in their hearts. But I think when I say these people are the kind that pray before, during, and after our trips—even saying grace before meals in public, of all things—that should paint the picture.

They were teaching me an important lesson. I was watching Christianity in action. I was learning that it is a twenty-four-hour-a-day, seven-day-a-week proposition. I felt increasingly comfortable with this group of people whom I would never have understood, much less joined, only a year or two before. One of the preachers who went with us to the prison on my first day said, "Religion is what we practice in our churches; what we practice here in the prisons and on the streets is Christianity." I was learning the difference.

We arrived in the large parking lot outside the massive buildings of the prison. It seemed it was more difficult to get into the prison than to get out. We left all our belongings save our driver's licenses in a locker. After being searched, going back and forth through a metal detector (the nails in our shoes could set it off), and signing various lists, we were ushered into the inner chambers of the prison.

We had to go through three heavy steel doors and one fierce-looking steel gate to get to the chapel. Once inside, I was immediately aware of the fact that it was not going to be easy to get out. My freedom, much like that of the prisoners, was totally dependent on the prison guards, or officers, as we call them.

Once there, I was surprised by what I saw. The chapel was a very large room with an altar, organ, and many trappings you or I would be happy to have in our own church. The room was filled with enough church pews to seat at least one hundred men. A modern slide projector flashed the words of hymns on a large screen in the front of the room. This was a real church—not just a leftover utility room like the one furnished at road camp.

Because I was going to play my banjo during our service, I was sitting up front, facing the congregation. By ten in the morning, the room was filled with convicts. Many looked very tough. I noticed there were no officers in chapel. There were about eighty convicts and ten of us, several of whom were women.

Just then, before my imagination started to play tricks, a young prisoner came to the front, faced the others and said, very firmly, "Praise the Lord!"

The room vibrated as the men responded in unison, "Praise the Lord!" Their arms were raised to the ceiling, to a man.

I felt a wave of the Holy Spirit surge through me that stayed with me throughout the day. These men sang, prayed, cried, laughed and listened as our two services (one in the morning, one in the afternoon) brought them the gospel. Later in the afternoon, we baptized five men in what looked like a fish pond in a little courtyard off the chapel. It was used as a baptismal font, but it could have doubled as a fish pond. These men were stripped to their undershorts and totally dunked three times by one of our members.

It was just a bit nippy that spring afternoon. I started to offer the less-drenching Episcopal pouring of water onto the head as an alternative. But when I saw how thrilled the men were to be baptized in the pond, I remained silent.

It was a glorious day for me. I was so Spirit-filled when I left the prison I knew it would last forever. Everyone on the team admitted it was a grand day. Besides the baptisms, we had twelve men come forward during the altar call to commit their lives to Christ. The depth of love some of the men displayed was inspiring.

These are men who are not going anywhere for a long time. They would get up and give their testimonies. Some said they were thankful to God for bringing them to prison. They told how they were sure they would have died on the streets without ever knowing Christ if they had not been put in prison. A glorious day, indeed. It was a glorious day.

The drive back home was filled with joy. Each person shared something different from the day. We compared miracles, so to speak. I learned how important it is for those of us who commit to go into the prisons to stick with it. The men count on seeing the same people each time. The conversion of a prisoner may take a long time. It may take many trips. When it happens it is absolutely stunning. Another man is then prepared to live in the godless atmosphere of the prison and make his stand for Jesus Christ.

My attitude was one of gratitude for being included in this faithful group. We were a mixed lot, from all segments of Christianity and diverse denominations. But we were united in our love for the prisoners and our opportunity to introduce them to our very best friend, Jesus. None of us was wealthy. In fact, most of us were struggling along from day to day. That was not important. It was not even noticed. Each person in that van knew wealth beyond compare that evening. It was so on each trip back from taking the reality of Jesus Christ to the prisoners.

10. Learning

Teach me to do thy will, for thou art my God! Let thy good spirit lead me on a level path!

Ps. 143:10

Driving to my barbershop on a fair day, the visit to the prison was replaying in my mind. Though it had been three weeks since my first visit to the big prison, I still felt spiritual excitement each time I thought of it. Plans were being made to go again in about two weeks. We tried to go to the big prison at least once a month and to the jail twice a month. Many times we would not know until the last minute if we were going to be allowed into the big prison. If any trouble started, there would be a lock-down, and we would not be allowed in that Saturday.

It occurred to me that it had been a few weeks since I had been involved with anyone with cancer. Maybe I was being led away from that ministry to the prison ministry. I decided to follow my best discernment of God's will. He would let me know what he wanted done, when he wanted it done, and how he wanted it done.

"Good morning, Ike," I said to my barber as I took off my coat, loosened my tie, and sank comfortably into the barber chair.

"Hi, Ken. How's it been going with you?"

Ike had been cutting my hair since the summer after my first bout with cancer. That was the summer of chemo-therapy and radiation treatments. I lost most of my hair. Ike's shop was near my office. One day I walked in un-announced. After telling him of my treatments to explain my almost bald condition, he gave me a very nice haircut. He is a pleasant man and a Christian.

It was not long until I discovered that Ike's daughter,

Cindy, was the young woman who had planned and executed my 32 radiation treatments that summer. I had thirty-two treatments over most of the summer. I was quite taken with Cindy because she witnessed to me unashamedly of her Christian faith. Her lovely recounting of God's love, I am sure, was one of the most important reasons my mood was good and my health was restored. Ike and I must always devote a little time to Cindy during my haircuts.

On that fine spring day four years after those treatments, Ike and I were generally passing the time of day. For most men my age a barbershop is a welcome retreat from the cares of the world. A good barber is a good conversationalist, maybe even a good psychiatrist. When one leaves his barbershop, the customer's head should feel better in more ways than one. Ike and I solved many of the world's problems during the course of one of my haircuts.

"Looks like I'm going to lose another customer to cancer," Ike said nonchalantly. Cancer was a common topic between us.

"That's too bad," I replied. "It seems like we are losing more and more. I sense medical science is close to a cure. It sure is a demonic disease."

"I doubt if you know this guy. He was in the sheriff's office." Ike was talking casually as he clipped along the back of my neck.

"I know quite a few law enforcement officers. What's his name, Ike?" I really did not think I would know him, I was mainly making small talk.

"His name is Ed Dana. Ever hear of him?" asked Ike.

I was stunned. There was a long silence as I gathered my thoughts.

"Ever hear of him, Ken?" Ike repeated.

"Ike, there's a lesson I learn over and over. I guess I can't remember it well enough, so God keeps teaching me. There is no such thing as coincidence. Do you realize that? There's absolutely no such an animal."

"Never gave it too much thought," Ike answered. "You know him, huh?"

I told Ike about my friendship with Ed Dana. I had worked with him twenty years before when I was in the public defender's office. Ed was the chief investigator. We were close friends, seeing each other on a daily basis for three years. I knew his beautiful young wife, Linda. I used to kid him about having a child bride, as she was ten years younger than Ed and I. I left the office to go into private practice, and our trails crossed less and less.

"Yep, Ike, I know Ed well. Just haven't seen him in about fifteen years. What kind of cancer does he have?"

"I'm not sure. I think it mainly has to do with the lungs. He's in St. Agnes Hospital now. Linda brought him in for a haircut about two weeks ago."

"You know, Ike, I think I'll go see him this afternoon. It will really surprise him. He may not even recognize me, it's been so long. I'm grateful to you for letting me know."

Ike finished my haircut. I paid him and left for the office to arrange things so I could go visit Ed in the hospital. There was no way I could know then that my entire manner of visiting people suffering from cancer was about to change 180 degrees. I was on the threshold of learning the essence of ministry to cancer patients.

After learning Ed's room number from the information desk, I proceeded to his room. I was familiar with that particular area of the hospital, the oncology floor. Walking into the room, I saw two beds. Ed's bed was the one farther from the door. A curtain hanging from a slider in the ceiling was drawn its full length between the beds. I could not see Ed immediately. At that moment, the bed nearer the door was not occupied.

A tall, well-dressed, distinguished man was just turning to leave. When he did, I saw Ed's wife, Linda, for the first time in more than fifteen years. Those years had only served to enhance her magnificent Nordic beauty, which at this time was only deepened by her sadness. She introduced me to Ernie, the man about to leave. He was a long-time family friend and at one time had been their pastor. We shook hands, and Ernie left the room.

Still, I was not into the room far enough to see Ed. I walked past the sliding curtain, gave Linda a brotherly hug, looked at Ed and walked to the side of his bed. We had not seen each other in at least fifteen years. He was very thin.

I shook his hand, and we started to visit. Linda excused herself, saying she had to go take care of the kids. They had two teenagers: Chris, 17, and Erin, 15. I had been so out of touch I did not know this.

During the years Ed and I worked together I knew him to be a rather angry man. He seldom expressed contentment with his job, his friends, or the world in general. He was able to express himself in a wryly humorous way, which softened his barbs a bit. Those of us who knew him well just took it as part of his personality. We used to kid him about his outlook. He was a curmudgeon, on the order of movie star and pianist Oscar Levant.

Talking in his hospital room I saw none of this quality had dissipated. He was now genuinely angry, mainly at himself. In a short while we were talking in depth. It was providential that Linda left when she did. Ed opened and betrayed some of his fears. His cancer involved the lungs. He had had it for almost two years. Through treatment he had been better for a few months, but it had now returned. He was given little, if any, hope at this point.

"I know I deserve this, Kenny. I brought it on myself with all those cigarettes. I just didn't think it was going to happen to me." His voice was weak and raspy. His remorse was profound.

"I see you were talking to your pastor. Are you a spiritual man? That's not how I remember you." I tried to humor him some. He was deeply depressed.

"Aw, you know, pal, I have a hard time with some of that stuff. I've gone to church pretty regularly with Linda and the kids, but there's just some of it I don't get."

"Does talking with your pastor, Ernie, help?" I was just making conversation, though I was interested in his spiritual life. I still had not reached the point where I would be intrusive about one's relationship with Christ. It did not seem right.

"Sometimes he makes me feel better. I just have a hard time swallowing some of what he says." Ed was in pain. He pushed a button, a nurse came and told him he could have some more medicine in exactly one hour.

I heard myself saying, "Ed, do you believe there was

an actual, historical man who walked this earth, named Jesus Christ?'' I was surprised I had initiated the subject that bluntly.

"Oh, yes, I do. No doubt about that.'' Ed was a keenly intelligent man, given to deep study of anything that puzzled him. "I have read a lot about him. That's not a problem.''

"Do you think Jesus is divine?'' I pressed.

"That I don't know about. But what difference does it make? Even if he is, he's not going to have anything to do with the likes of me.'' Tears began to form in Ed's eyes.

"Why do you say that, my friend?'' I asked.

"I have to be the world's greatest sinner. What does he want with me? I don't deserve him. That's what I can't tell Pastor Ernie. There's no way Jesus would have anything to do with me—even if he is God's son.'' The tears were flowing down his face now. I really did not know what to do.

"Ed, I want to tell you something. I believe with all my heart that Jesus Christ is exactly who he says he is. There's no doubt about it. If I have any credibility in your eyes, that should get you to thinking.'' He listened raptly.

I told him of my experience with cancer. He had not heard about it. He was incredulous as I told him where I had been. I gave him one of my books. We talked for about thirty more minutes. His tears were gone and he was paying close attention.

"I better go now, Ed. Would you be offended by a short prayer?'' I was again acting against my usual form.

"I'd really like that, Ken,'' said Ed, surprising me.

"Before we pray I want to assure you that you and I are just who Jesus is looking for. I'm sure I can match you story for story as to who's the greatest sinner. You know my life was not lily-white. Jesus is looking for you and me and other sinners. He loves us. He doesn't need to look for the ones who are not sinning, whoever they are. Are you familiar with St. Paul?''

"Very definitely, I am.'' said Ed.

"You remember, Paul said somewhere in the Bible that He knew Christ came to save sinners and that he, Paul, was the foremost sinner of them all.''

"I remember that. I have heard it many times. But that was long ago." Ed was still doubtful.

"Let's pray now, Ed." I got up and took his hand in mine. I did not know what he would think of that. He was comfortable with it. I prayed a short prayer only because I could not think of much else to say. I prayed a version of what we call the sinners prayer in the prisons.

"Dear Lord. Help your servant Ed to open his heart to the reality of your Son, Jesus Christ. Help Ed to ask him into his heart even if he has doubts. Help Ed to pray for Jesus to come into his life even if he doesn't believe. And God, we know your will for Ed is health. Make Ed well according to your will. We ask this in Christ's name. Amen."

I squeezed Ed's hand, told him I had to go, and left. As I walked to my car I was really berating myself for being so firm with Ed about his religion. After all, I had not seen him in fifteen years and had no idea where he stood in that respect.

I remember clearly saying to myself, "What a stupid prayer. You sounded like you couldn't even speak English."

The Lord gently let me know that the prayer was fine. It said all it had to say. When I thought about it, I realized it did. We don't have to speak the King's English to get through to the Lord. Praise the Lord!

The next afternoon as I walked into Ed's room, he was alone and dozing. When he saw me a broad smile came across his skinny face.

"Hey, pal. It worked. It really worked." He was excited about something.

"What worked?" I asked, really not knowing.

"Jesus came into my heart last night. He loves me. He's real and he's mine. It really worked, Kenny. Everything is fine now."

"Praise the Lord!" I said forcefully. "I guess he heard our prayers."

We visited for a spell, basking in the warmth of Ed's new-found conversion. I learned he was going home the next day. We said some prayers of thanksgiving, and I left. I told him I would be in touch.

"Hey, pal. Thanks. You hear? Thanks."

I did not know exactly what I had done. Being somewhat puzzled I said, "You're welcome, pal. You're welcome. I'll see you later."

Driving out of the hospital parking lot I was crying with happiness at actually seeing God's mighty work in action. I knew then I was never going to pussyfoot around with a person who could be dying, or anyone else for that matter, when it came to witnessing that Jesus Christ is the only way. If the person wants to reject the message, that is between that person and God.

I have since learned how to handle any anger I arouse by doing this hard-sell ministry, if that is what it is. To be truthful, I have only had one or two reject what I had to say. I try to do it in a nonoffensive way, but I do it. If someone seems upset I simply say that when we are both in line on Judgment Day with me on one side of the fence and him or her on the other, I don't want to hear anyone asking me, "Why didn't you tell me?" Praise God!

11. Grief

But when they rise from the dead, they neither marry nor are given in marriage, but are like angels in heaven.

Mark 12:25

While Ed was at home I visited him at least three or four times each week. He knew he was not long for this world. He slipped noticeably, but slowly, daily. He was surrounded by Linda, his teenage son and daughter, his older son, Mike, and Linda's mother, Lillian. His care was supportive and spoke persuasively about the value of dying at home, if at all possible.

During my visits I spent almost all of the time with Ed. We talked about all kinds of things: old friends, old enemies, problems with our jobs, and other things we shared in common. Not a visit would go by that Ed did not have a question about his spiritual voyage. We would look up the answers in the Bible, and I was pleased to watch his joy in finding his problems addressed in Scripture.

He had no fear. He was completely absorbed in the fact that he would be home with the Lord in the not-too-distant future. He was in pain, but the medication was working satisfactorily to control it. At the close of each visit Ed asked me to pray with him. Together we prayed for healing, we prayed for strength and courage to do whatever it was God wanted him to do. We gave prayers of thanksgiving for the healing that was taking place in Ed's spirit. It was astounding.

On one of my last visits another of God's not-so-subtle assurances of his reality unfolded. As I approached the front door of Ed and Linda's home, Dennis, an old friend of both mine and Ed's from the days of the public defender's office, was coming out. Dennis and his wife, Robbie, and Ed and

Linda had been the very best of friends for twenty years, at least. Dennis was a superior court judge. Through that, I maintained contact with him. It had been several years since I had seen Dennis.

Dennis stopped to talk. As he looked at me he shook his head in disbelief. I thought Ed had taken a turn for the worse or even died.

"I don't believe it. I've never seen anything like this before in my life," Dennis said, looking at me, as if for the answer.

"What happened?" I asked.

"I've known that man for many years. I have never seen him like this." He still shook his head.

"Like what? What's happened?" I had no idea what was happening.

"He's calm. He's cool. He has no fear. He knows he's dying, but he is not afraid. He treats everyone with love. That's not the old Ed we know, Ken. What happened?"

I relaxed and smiled; "Dennis, you have witnessed the grand miracle that happens when we ask Christ into our lives. Ed's situation is more drastic, maybe that's why it shows more. It happened while he was still in the hospital. That surely should be proof enough for anyone that God's promises are real." Here I was, evangelizing the judge.

"I've watched Ed closely," Dennis continued. "I've tried to find some flaw of self-pity, some bitterness or hate. It's just not there. Ed is loving and well adjusted. It doesn't seem to bother him that death is coming." Dennis told me he would talk with me later and walked off to his car, still shaking his head.

That moment was one of my most thrilling, measured in terms of "being in on" a dramatic conversion. I felt God had included me in this one, and I must admit I relished the thought.

When I got inside the house I saw Ed was up on the sun porch, sitting in his wheel chair, entertaining several of his friends. I did not know any of them. His eyes were bright and he was laughing and kidding around with everyone. The others were not doing a very good job of hiding the fact they knew the end was near. It's hard. It is very hard to maintain a normal, objective attitude when we deal with a loved one we know is dying. I cannot do it well, even though I believe with all my heart that going to be with God is part of the essence of our existence.

Linda met me at the door. We spent a few minutes at the front of the house visiting before I went in to see Ed and meet the other folks. Since the beginning of my involvement in their lives, Linda exhibited an extraordinary bravery. Every time I saw her, she was totally composed. It became obvious she was a woman of undiluted spirituality and faith. These were the qualities that carried her through the ordeal of watching the man she loved pass on into the next life.

Linda's strength was such that I found myself drawing on it as a source of courage before I would go in to see Ed. I did not see this all at once on our first visit. It came to me a little each time I talked with Linda. She saw that the house ran as smoothly as it could and that Erin's and Chris's lives continued exactly on course. They are both honor students in accelerated programs. From all I could see, they hardly missed a step.

Because of Linda's obvious strength, I did not spend much time visiting with her. Almost all my time was spent with Ed. On occasion she would join us for a few minutes. It gave me the opportunity, again, to rib him about his child bride.

"You're just lucky you met her before I did," I would kid. "A beautiful woman like that belongs with a guy like me, not you."

Ed would laugh out loud and that would set the tone for another light-hearted visit. When I would leave, Linda would escort me to the door and tell me how much my visits meant to Ed. I continued to assure her that God could reverse the situation. We both knew he could. Linda did not act as if she thought he would. At this point Ed had suffered with cancer for two years.

There were one or two more visits, each much like those before. The last time I walked out of the Danas' house, Linda and I had a short talk about heaven and the fact that, should Ed die now, they would one day be together again with the Lord. Again, her display of courage was touching. I apologized for not having spent more time with her. She assured me she knew Ed needed my time more than she did.

"I'll call you tomorrow. It's Thursday. I'll try to get by Saturday morning." I gave her a slight hug around the shoulders and turned to leave.

"OK, Ken. Don't feel like you have to be over here all the time," she said. "But know that we really appreciate it."

"No problem. I really look forward to it, Linda. Don't ask me why, but I really do. I'll see you Saturday." I got in my car and headed home.

Saturday morning I was up having my coffee and reading the paper—one of my rituals, if the world allows it. It was fairly early, around nine o'clock. The phone rang.

I picked it up and lazily said, "Hello."

"Ken. This is Linda. You don't have to come over this morning."

I knew instinctively what it was.

"Ed's gone?" I asked, already knowing the answer.

"Yes. He's gone." I could tell she was sad, but there was also a note of relief in her voice.

"God bless him. This is a blessing. You know how I feel this is God's ultimate healing." We had discussed these things during my visits with Ed. Ed felt the same way.

"Yes, and I agree." Linda seemed to be planning all the last details as we talked.

"Is there anything I can do for you, Linda?" I asked.

"No, Ken. You've done so much already. There are plenty of family and friends. Mike and Annette are here and so's my mom. We'll be fine. Thank you again, Ken." (Mike is Ed's oldest son by a prior marriage. Annette is Mike's charming young wife of just a year or so.)

We chatted briefly, and I told Linda good-bye. After hanging up, I, too, felt a certain sense of conclusion. I thought a moment about the fact that Linda had not given the details of the funeral. As I mulled it over, I knew I probably would not go to the funeral anyway. After all, until that fateful day in the barbershop I had not given much thought to Ed Dana for many years. It seemed our paths crossed solely to teach me the importance of being firm and truthful about one's witnessing and to be used in Ed's conversion. I learned not to pass up any opportunities. Don't cast your pearls before swine, but don't drop the ball. Don't blow it.

My younger sister, Martha, died at the age of 37 in 1972. She had cancer. About a month before she died, I had flown back to Albuquerque, New Mexico, to be with her for several days. On her death, after talking with my mother, I decided I would not fly back again for her funeral. Mother did not want me there; it was too sad for her. There were many relatives to comfort her. I knew there was nothing more I could do for Martha. It all went well. If I can be of help to those who remain, I will attend the services. I believe the deceased has gone on to be with God.

I have followed that philosophy since that time. Once or twice a close friend has lost a child or a loved one and requested me to sit with the family at the funeral. I have and have felt that was where I belonged. My generation went to funerals just to be seen and to see. When I was a boy in west Texas, it seemed people went to funerals almost as others went to movies. I know funerals have a purpose in helping the bereaved. But unless I am one of the bereaved, I simply do not go.

That was the last I heard from any of the Dana family for quite some time. We prayed prayers for the faithful departed in our services at my church. I told him farewell and turned Ed over to God. That was April 1987.

The next month to six weeks ran fairly normally. I was busy with my work. Diana, my fiancée became interested in some of the prison ministry. She said she was not quite ready to go to the big prison, but she wanted to go along on our trips to the jail. She played classical guitar exceptionally well, having studied in Spain under Segovia. She wondered if her style of guitar would be something the men at the jail would like.

One Sunday night several of us took off in the van for the jail. Diana was with us. She was looking forward to the evening. She said she was going to size up the men and decide about playing for them. She was working up some beautiful arrangements of some popular old hymns. If she thought they would like them, the next time she would bring the guitar and play for them.

This particular evening, about mid-May, was one of the outstanding meetings. The men responded to all of us and our service with remarkable intensity. We had about thirty minutes after the service to have one-on-one counseling and prayer with those who desired it. It was a good evening. Diana responded to it as I thought she would. She loved it. She wanted to become a regular. She told us she was going to bring the guitar the next time. I was so pleased that she liked the ministry. Up until then, the time I spent going to the prisons was time we were apart. Neither of us liked that.

Diana had a little home up in the mountains, about two hours from Fresno. She loved it. I loved it in the summer when there was no snow. That was the time of the year we really enjoyed her cabin. We would take our respective kids and grandkids (we each had prior marriages), up several weekends a season. We shared this spot with our friends on other weekends. We would just sit around playing games, visiting, and cooking huge meals. It was a wonderful place for all to enjoy.

During the month of May, we attended and enjoyed a couple of banjo events. I was not involved with anyone dying with cancer, or anyone getting over cancer for that matter. It was a good month for Diana and me. We had more time to do some of the things we enjoyed doing together. And we took advantage of it. We even made a couple of tapes of Diana on one side and me on the other for some of our out-of-town musician friends. Most every night we would enjoy dinner together, either out or at her house or mine.

Our respective responsibilities to our families and my cancer and its recurrence had made it difficult for us to set a definite date to get married. It was a major topic of conversation in 1987 as we thought we were just about to see daylight. We were talking very seriously about two things that May—marriage and a cruise to Alaska. Each had been a dream of ours for at least four years. Now, we thought, we might be able to pull it off.

In early June we attended a big Dixieland festival, having a wonderful time. I was playing banjo in one of the bands, and Diana was out strolling through the shops. She was in and out, first shopping, then listening. We had done this on several like occasions in prior years. She seemed to be more relaxed at this one. She really enjoyed the outing. Diana was raising her eight-year old granddaughter, Jennifer, and was fully responsible for the care of her twenty-four-year-old son, Wally, who is almost completely paralyzed from an accident he suffered when he was sixteen.

We were happy. The things we shared together, we enjoyed. The things we did apart from each other, we enjoyed sharing. Everything seemed to be going along smoothly. It was almost two years since my last surgery. That was a pretty good sign. My doctor said that if problems were going to come back, they generally came back in the first year or so. I was feeling very well and content with my lot.

On June 17, 1987, I was scheduled to go to trial in a town about fifty miles from Fresno. Many times when I go out of town, my mother enjoys riding along with me. We left early, as the trial was to start at ten in the morning. It was a nice day for a drive down the valley. The vegetation produced by the prodigious farming done there was beautiful and inspiring.

We arrived at the courthouse about nine-thirty. Mother said she would wait in the car until I found out if I was going to get to trial. I went into the courtroom and learned that it was highly unlikely a courtroom would be available. When the bailiff found out who I was, he told me the clerk had an important message for me. I retrieved it. It said to call my office—there had been an emergency.

Finding the nearest phone, I called. My secretary, Joanne, answered and said, "Sunshine called." Sunshine is Diana's youngest daughter—a lovely girl and Diana's pride and joy. "She said Diana is in the hospital. They will be taking her off life support in a few hours." That was all she knew. "Something like a stroke, I guess," Joanne said, finishing the conversation from her side. I told her I would see her when I saw her. I was not going to trial since we had no courtroom. I was going straight to the hospital and would check in when I found out what was going on.

Mother and I drove back to Fresno. I dropped Mother off at home and went to the hospital. I found that Diana was in a unit similar to the cardiac arrest unit. Sunshine was near the entrance to this unit as I entered. We gave each other a big hug, and she took me into a room where many members of Diana's family were listening to a preacher. Diana's mother and father, and her son, Wally, in his wheelchair were there. Also present were Walt, her former husband and the father of her children; Sunshine's husband, Dave; and one or two other people. Her other children, Dan and Laura, lived out of town. Everyone, of course, was in total shock.

On the previous afternoon, Diana had suffered a broken blood vessel in her brain while hiking up near her home in the mountains. She lost consciousness about an hour later. She was brought down the hill, to the hospital where she continued to show vital signs until about eight o'clock on this particular morning. Since she had donated her organs, the doctors wanted to perform surgery later in the day to remove them. In the meantime, they kept her hooked up to various machines.

Walt, a dentist, told me he had seen the X-rays and talked to the doctors. It was a massive stroke. I was numb. There was nothing for me to do or say. A verse from Psalm 116 came to mind, and I feebly shared it with the gathered family. "Precious in the sight of the Lord is the death of his saints" (Ps. 116:15). I don't know if it helped them. I know it helped me.

I told everyone I would be in touch and left the room. Alberta, Diana's mother, asked if I wanted to see Diana. I did. She took me into the room. Diana was stretched out on the bed, still looking as though she were sleeping. Her eyes were closed and had tape over them. Even though the machine kept her breathing, I knew she was gone. I cried. I cried for several minutes.

While I stood by her, holding her cooling hand and crying, a sermon I had heard way in the past came to mind. The preacher was telling of when Jesus called Lazarus from the tomb. He explained the Jews of those days believed that a person's spirit hovered around the body for up to four days after death. That is why Jesus waited four days before calling Lazarus back to life. He wanted everyone to be certain Lazarus was dead before he performed his miracle.

At that moment, though my brain told me Diana was dead, my heart and soul told me her spirit was still present. I placed my final kiss on her beautiful forehead, said, "Goodbye, Sweetheart, I'll see you soon," and left after embracing all the family members who were still around.

I went home and told mother that Diana was gone. We both cried some and talked some. Mother has lost almost everyone dear to her in this life. At 85, grief of this type was nothing new to her. I went to the office, as I knew from experience it helps to stay busy at times like this. I knew then, as I know even more now, I had just lost my very best friend. I did not know how I was going to handle it.

Diana died nine months ago. My faith in God and his promises has been a tremendous help through the grief process. My grief for Diana is too young, too raw, for me to be able to offer any earthshaking insights into dealing with a loss of a dear loved one. But I will share some things that have been of help to me, in the hope that others will find them helpful, too. I probably don't have anything new or novel. Grief is something that has to be gone through. We cannot go around it, under it, or over it. This is all I know for certain as I write this. God helps us through it. We can make it with God.

12. Retreat

He makes me lie down in green pastures. He leads me beside still waters; he restores my soul.

Ps. 23:2, 3a

"Let's stop and get a few donuts for the road, maybe a little coffee." I was doing the driving, and I like to have a little sustenance along the way.

"I'll take some coffee. I don't want any donuts," said my mother. Since I can remember, most of us refer to Mother as Mo.

"I'd better get you a couple anyway, just to keep you from eating mine." We laughed. I stopped and got a sack of donuts and two styrofoam cups of hot coffee.

Mo and I were off on one of our famous trips. It was the first week in July 1987, barely two weeks after Diana's going to be with God. My mood was still one of shock. I had lost friends and relatives, all of whom I loved deeply. This was the first time I had lost a person who held the position in my heart and soul that was exclusively Diana's for over five years. I was handling it as well as could be expected, outwardly. Inside, I was lost and confused and my very being was heavy with grief and disbelief.

Mo and I decided I might as well take my vacation early and drive her back to New Mexico and Colorado to see some of our relatives. At that point, it made little difference to me what I did. I remembered how much the trip Mo and I made back that way in 1983 had helped. I figured I couldn't lose anything. I enjoy driving and traveling. I knew it would make Mo happy and get me away from the situation. So, off we went.

We enjoy seeing relatives in Albuquerque. At least we had a good visit and a Mexican dinner down in Old Town.

We lived in that lovely city for two years in the early forties, so it is fun to drive around and see the old places. The main object of the trip as far as mother was concerned was Denver. Here my late sister Martha's two daughters, Beverly and Becky live with their husbands and children. Ched, Martha's husband and the girls' father, and Wendy, his wife, and their two young ones live outside Denver. Our relations with Ched and Wendy are extremely good, though it has been over fifteen years since Martha died.

Seeing Mo around her great-grandchildren was worth the trip. The Senate hearings with Oliver North were on during most of the time we were gone. We would drive along visiting and enjoying the scenery and listening to the hearings over the radio.

We traversed some of the same highways I traveled in 1985 after the General Convention, and in 1983, prior to my first surgery. It still had an eerie effect on me. Here I was, four years later. That was easily two years more than anyone gave me at the outset. The landscape throughout Arizona, New Mexico, and Colorado is so breathtaking one is given little choice save to praise God on a minute-by-minute basis. We drove home from Denver through the southern part of Utah—down through St. George, the Virgin River Gorge, and on to Las Vegas and home. Awesome, totally awesome, as the kids say.

We were gone ten days. It was a wonderful opportunity for me to view my situation at home with some distance added. We talked at length about Diana, death, and grief. When all is said and done, there is not much that can be said or done by anyone other than the person going through it. During the trip I was heavily into a stage of grief I described as, "I wish I hadn't said that," or "I wish I hadn't done that," also known as "I wish I had done that." It goes in circles.

Time is the main cure—time, a great deal of prayer, and trying to keep occupied. As I said earlier, I am still going through the process. Therefore, I do not want to spend much time here trying to define grief. Several things have been very helpful. I read the Scriptures, talked to priests, and did quite a bit of reading on what happens when

Christians die. I am totally convinced we go to be with God.

The concept of the Communion of Saints is comforting. The believers who have passed on and those who remain have a communion with each other and with God. Even though Diana and I each had prior marriages, the relationship we will have in heaven will be glorious. We, and all in heaven, will be as angels. I know from the Word that we will have an inconceivably wonderful friendship in heaven. It is what we had here that I miss in my sad moments.

Something I felt strongly when it happened gets stronger as time passes. I feel God sent for Diana. Her burdens were many, and she handled them valiantly. At the moment of her stroke she was at her favorite place in the world—her home in the mountains. She was doing what she loved most—hiking in those mountains. She was taken quickly and, as far as we know, painlessly. We should all be similarly blessed.

Diana's daughter Sunshine, God bless her, has been ever so solicitous of my feelings, as I have tried to be of hers. This mutual concern has helped us both. I was included in decisions that meant a great deal to me, such as choosing and helping to design the headstone for Diana's grave. I was asked to advise on many things concerning the details of Diana's affairs. This helped.

One last thing I can share that was a balm to my grieving soul is one that fell into my lap. Diana was very fond of the Grand Canyon. She made several trips into the canyon on foot and otherwise. She was planning a hiking trip into the canyon in September 1987. Upon inquiry, I found I could make a donation in her memory to the Grand Canyon National Park. I did, designating that it go for planting trees or something permanent. It worked out beautifully. Now her family and I know there is a living memorial to her in her beloved Grand Canyon. They sent us a certificate to prove it.

Many of these thoughts occurred to me on our trip. Some have come to me since. Grief, at least mine, is a slow but steady process. By the time we returned to Fresno, I felt things were coming under control.

There were still several days of my vacation left. I dropped Mo off in Fresno and headed for Santa Barbara and Mount Calvary Retreat House. I knew some time down there would be healthy. My good friend from the church, Frank Wright, and I spent three renewing and soul-restoring days with the good brothers. By the time we came back to Fresno, I felt ready to resume my duties. It was the first time I had felt that way since Diana's sudden death.

Life was slowly falling back into place. Things were getting back to normal. I was able to laugh a little more easily. I was able to enjoy being with other people, one of my favorite pastimes, and my music was becoming fun again. While I still hurt, sometimes more than others, I knew I would heal. As with my cancer, I knew there would be some scarring.

During the first week of August, after I was somewhat back in the swing of things at the office, I got a call from Hope, in Dr. Felix's office. Hope is the lovely woman who has been so much help ever since the first surgery. Over the years we have developed a nice rapport. She was reminding me it was time for my routine blood tests, lung X-rays, and CT scan. This helped shake me back to earth. I realized I had not given my cancer any thought since Diana died.

It took three or four days to give the tests and receive the results. When they have everything, they normally have me come in for a visit. This time it was no different. Hope called and made an appointment.

After the usual preliminaries, I ended up in the examining room to wait for Dr. Felix. Everyone was cheerful and pleasant. It was routine.

Suddenly, Dr. Felix stuck his head in the door and asked if it would be all right if he saw me last. He only had two more patients to see, and he'd like to be able to spend some time with me. That did not bother me, so I agreed. This resulted in a twenty-minute wait. I waited, staring at the walls. It never occurred to me what was coming next.

At last, Dr. Felix entered the room and took a seat on one of those little round stools that spin up and down. He had my chart with him. By now it was pretty thick. He was affable enough.

"There's something growing at the site of the original tumor. I don't like it. We will have to go get it." Dr. Felix is a man of few words in circumstances like these.

Pow! I felt as though the other shoe had dropped, only it was a seven-league boot. I was dumbfounded.

"I'm afraid it's a return of the old leiomyosarcoma, though I won't know until I get in there. If it is, I don't think we can cure it. We might be able to get you another three or four years. It's very near your remaining kidney. You might lose it." He was letting me have it all at once. It was the only way for me to deal with it.

I was scared. I found myself being more afraid of living without kidneys than I was of dying. I had no choice.

My mood was best described by my favorite scene from a good movie, *Butch Cassidy and the Sundance Kid.* Butch and the Kid are standing with their horses on a ledge of a canyon. It is 200 feet down to the river. The posse is hard behind them.

"Only one way out. We have to jump," Butch says.

"But I can't swim," whines the Kid.

"Don't worry, Sundance, the fall will probably kill you," Butch says with a grin just before jumping.

By now I had developed the firm opinion that part of God's intervention in my case was getting me into the hands of the very finest doctors. I never even entertained the thought of not following Dr. Felix's advice.

"Let's get it over with," I said, knowing he was going to anyway.

We walked out to Hope's desk and the necessary details were arranged. I was scheduled for surgery in ten days. I left the office, back on square one, as far as being in shock was concerned. I spent the time before surgery working at the office and trying to find out all I could about dialysis. I prayed almost constantly, in one form or another. Several days before I was to go in the hospital, Dr. Felix told me I had only a 10 percent chance of losing the kidney. I felt better, but I was scared.

My fears were subsiding more quickly than prior to previous operations. My faith was stronger, I guess. I will admit this new twist alleviated my preoccupation with the loss of Diana, though I missed terribly having her near me to help me through the crisis as she had always done before. I was nervous.

The Saturday immediately before my surgery—scheduled for Monday—was a big prison day. I was getting jittery, and I was on a liquid diet in preparation for the surgery. I had decided I would not try to make the trip to the prison. Friday evening I received a call asking if I was going to the prison. In a split second I changed my mind and said, "Sure. Why not? I need to get my mind off my troubles. I'll see you in the morning."

When I start to talk about Providence to some of my friends, I get funny looks. Here is what happened. I had long since said to the Lord, "Thy will be done." I meant it, but I was still afraid of losing my only kidney. I was still the same old coward I had always been. Any strength I felt must have come from God. I had none.

Early Saturday morning our team took off for the big prison. During the course of the day we conducted two services and five baptisms. After we finished all that, about four in the afternoon, the chaplain of the prison called me forward. He knew of my upcoming operation. He's a powerful man for the Lord in that milieu. He explained to the eighty-some convicts what was happening. He called for prayer for healing.

The chaplain's prayer must have lasted twenty minutes or more. During the course of that prayer, every prisoner in the chapel came up and laid hands on me. At one time there must have been forty pairs of hands. It was hard to remain standing.

I felt a powerful surge of the Holy Spirit in that room. When the prayer was over and all the men had returned to the pews, I thanked them.

"I know this," I said uncharacteristically. "Whatever happens in that operating room, I know I am healed. Praise the Lord!"

From that very moment on I was without fear or anxiety. I could not explain it to anyone who does not believe in God's healing grace. God had prepared me, through the hands of those condemned men, to face whatever was to come. It was exhilarating.

An insight began to germinate in my mind and soul. It would be months before I would feel its full impact. Suddenly, I felt a strong kinship with these men—these prisoners. I sensed a brotherhood I could not describe.

Over the ensuing months, as I prayed with more and more convicts, both one-on-one and from the podium, I realized cancer patients are, themselves, prisoners. They are captive to fear, physical disability, and agendas over which they have no control. I now talk brother-to-brother to the men behind bars.

After the prayers of those men, God's plans for me were no longer questions bothering me. I was ready. This is not to say that I am not a worldly man. I am. I love it here. I am a vain man, and I want to enjoy perfect health and a strong appearance. My faith in my Lord covers a broad spectrum of intensity at different times. Many times I remove myself far from him. In view of the above, though, what can I say? God must give me the faith and strength to do his will. I know one thing—he will and he does. Praise the Lord, again and again!

13. Faith

Take heart, daughter, your faith has made you well. . . .
Matt. 9:22b

Here I was, back in my big chair, having been home from the hospital only two days. I knew from prior experience that I was in for several weeks of recuperation and then several months of diminished strength.

My surgery had been successful. I still had my kidney. My worst fears were for naught. It seems to be that way most of the time. I was looking at my new scar, remembering a funny conversation Dr. Felix and I had had after my second operation. Dr. Felix is Jewish—by his own words more cultural than religious. As he listens to all my Christian talk he sometimes smiles gently and goes on about his business.

The scar from my first operation runs over two feet from just under my left breast, over the navel and around my right side to my back. It runs parallel to the ground. It is long and prominent. When I was being examined for the second surgery, two years later, Dr. Felix said he was going to make the incision along the old scar. That way I would have only one scar.

When I came to, after the second surgery, I saw that my new scar ran up and down, from between my breasts almost to my groin. This one was perpendicular to the former one. When I questioned Dr. Felix about this he grinned and said, "I knew you would want a cross on your belly." We have had some laughs about that.

On the third and most recent operation, Dr. Felix did what he was going to do the second time; he ran the incision along the scar from the first surgery. It left me with two scars and three operations.

"I didn't want to mess up your cross, Ken," Dr. Felix kidded just an hour or so after my third surgery.

"Whew!" I joked, still very groggy from the anesthesia. "I was afraid I was going to end up with the Star of David carved into my beautiful body." We all had a good laugh.

While I sat in my big chair reviewing that colloquy, I was a thankful man. Getting over surgery was becoming a familiar experience. I knew that with care and exercise I would probably be back at my office in about three weeks. I knew it would take six months or so to feel 100 percent. I had been there before. After my first surgery, these last two were cakewalks. I thanked God for keeping me around some more. I replayed the words of Dr. Felix, recounting what he found.

"You did have a leiomyosarcoma. It had come back. It was not very large; we got it early. This time it was on the duodenum. That is the first part of your small intestine. It is exactly where I would have predicted it would come back, if it did. That's a good sign, for it to recur at the site of highest risk rather than somewhere else. I was able to get it all, along with a healthy amount of good tissue. Your kidney is fine. You'll be around awhile."

This was good news after all the worry about losing the kidney. God's healing either came in sets, or it was a continuing thing. It hardly made any difference. I was still here and well. I had been winged a time or two, but after time passed, I would be back on my feet.

On the morning I was discharged from the hospital, Dr. Felix was taking the stitches out of my incision.

"You know, Ken. It took that tumor almost five years to come back. It came back at the most predictable place and was very small for that length of time. That's all good news. I would give you a fifty-fifty chance of a cure."

That was good to hear from a man not given to making predictions. I know his is only a very educated guess, but it is comforting.

These things were going through my mind, making me feel a bit elated. I had been home only three days. It would be at least another two weeks before I could return to work. A ring of the phone next to my chair broke the spell. I answered.

"Ken, this is Linda. Linda Dana."

I was pleased to hear from her. She had been on my mind lately.

"Linda, how in the world are you? It's funny you should call. I have been giving serious thought to calling you. Did you hear Diana died a little over two months ago?"

"No, I hadn't heard that. I'm terribly sorry, Ken. I know how much she meant to you. I'm sorry."

After briefly giving her the details, I continued.

"Several times I wanted to call you to see if you might like to go to dinner or something. I didn't know if you were quite ready, and I didn't know if I could handle it either."

"I wish you had called. I would have liked that," Linda said sincerely.

"Well, nothing says we can't do it now," said I, beginning to feel enthusiastic about the project.

"Maybe so, Ken. But I'm calling from St. Agnes Hospital. I am going into surgery in the morning."

"What on earth for, Linda?" I asked with astonishment. My memory of Linda was as a healthy and strong woman. Very pretty and mighty strong I recalled. She was a young, vibrant 45.

"Cancer. We'll find out where and how much tomorrow." I could hear the anxiety in her voice. I knew what she was going through.

"Linda, would you like me to come see you now?" I asked. "There is no way you would know this, but I just came home from the hospital. I had more surgery about ten days ago."

"I didn't know, Ken. What was it?"

"My original cancer came back, but we got it."

"Are you sure you feel like coming over? That's pretty soon after your operation."

"I wouldn't miss it for the world. I'm on my way. I can use the exercise."

"I would really like to see you, Ken. Come over just as soon as you can."

We hung up. I changed clothes and left for the hospital. I was still pretty weak, so I had to move slowly. I parked at the spot closest to the building where Linda's room was

located. Still I had about a fifty-yard walk to the elevator.
I took it slow and easy. I remember thinking that if Linda
stayed very long, I would get most of my walking in by
coming to see her.

This was the same floor of the same hospital where
Linda's husband, Ed, had been prior to his death. I knew
all the nurses and several of the doctors. I had spent so much
time on that floor I think some of the employees thought
I was either a doctor or a preacher. I found Linda's room.

She was sitting on the edge of the made-up bed looking
radiant. This being the afternoon prior to her surgery, she
had not gotten into hospital garb and was mainly receiving
some visitors and waiting. She was nicely dressed and was
very cheerful.

We had an hour or two that afternoon without any other
friends or relatives around. It gave us ample opportunity
to discuss what was going to happen and what to expect.
Having just gone through Ed's experience, Linda was knowledgeable about the whole hospital procedure.

She wanted to pray. We prayed several times during the
course of that afternoon. It did not take long for me to find
that the faith I had noticed during Ed's ordeal was real and
firm. In fact, if anything, her faith had grown since I last
talked to her. There was no need to talk to Linda about
Christ; she was beginning to teach me a thing or two.

All that was known was that she had ovarian cancer.
She told me she had no warning at all. Over the years, she
had had all the tests currently expected of women. There
was no hint. Nothing had been going on that was abnormal.
She was more mad than anything else. Her doctor, Dr.
Medrano, had been Ed's doctor. I had gotten to know him
through the experiences of several of my friends. He is a
good and caring doctor.

The doctors and hospital personnel expressed shock at
the stark coincidence of two cancers in the same family
within months. Through Ed's illness everyone became
acquainted with all the family members and friends of the
Danas. It was a sad thing. Linda was somehow above the
pathos surrounding her plight. Hers was an attitude of wait
and see.

I told her I'd see her after her surgery the next day.

"Hurry up and get this behind you," I said. "Don't forget, we've a heavy date for dinner."

"You're right, Ken. We'll do it before too long."

Walking to the car, I was really looking forward to having dinner with Linda. Linda, I thought, would be a nice person to get to know better. I remember telling her one time that I was sure even Ed and Diana would approve of our seeing each other. She agreed.

The next day I was there as Linda was coming out of surgery. The news was not good. Her cancer had spread to and severely involved a large portion of her liver. I could not understand how it could have advanced so far, so quickly, without her knowing it. Then I remembered my first cancer. It was within about a month of killing me— and about the size of a basketball—when I had my surgery.

The next two months were spent with Linda on an almost daily basis. She was in and out of the hospital. I visited with her there and at home. It was not too long before we received more bad news: Linda also had some tumors in her brain. She underwent a series of both chemotherapy and radiation treatments simultaneously. She had good days and bad. Toward the end she had more bad than good.

Throughout this ordeal, her faith in God shone constantly. There was never a whimper. She said many times that no matter what happened, she won. We prayed each visit. If I would start to leave without a prayer, she would remind me. Even at the very last, when she could barely talk, I could not get out of her room without holding her hand and praying.

Linda took everything they threw at her. She was ready if she got well, and she was ready if the Lord wanted her home. I have seen few faiths as brilliant and strong as Linda's. It was a witness to all who saw her.

On the next to last day, I walked into her room at the hospital. She was in a semiconscious state. When I walked up to the bed she opened her eyes and looked at me.

"I'm very tired," she said. Her mother, Lillian, was in the room with us. "What do I do now?" asked Linda.

"You mean you're tired of fighting?" I asked.

"Yes," she said. It was difficult for her to talk.

"What you do now is between you and God." I said. "If you want to go be with God, and Ed, I'm sure you'll be welcomed with open arms. If you want to stay and fight, that's probably all right, too." She went back to sleep. Lillian and I talked awhile, then I left.

The next day I went to see Linda. Lillian was there, as usual.

"Do you know what she told me this morning, Ken? It is the last thing she said." Lillian was touched. She, too, is a profoundly Christian woman.

"What did she say?" I asked. Linda was in a coma.

"She said that this morning, early, Jesus Christ had come into the room and talked to her. She pointed over to that part of the room and said that's where Jesus was. He told her he was going to take her home. She was so serene and peaceful. What do you think, Ken?"

"If she said Jesus came to see her, I believe he came to see her. Now she is on a different plane than we are. Of course, I believe he was here."

"So do I," said Lillian.

At that moment there was a cloudburst all over the north part of Fresno, the area where the hospital is located. A double rainbow formed. The wind carried it exactly in the direction of Linda's room. It evaporated just before coming over the building.

"What do you think of that, Ken?" Lillian asked.

"That is God's promise to us, isn't it?" I answered.

"That's right. That is God's promise." Lillian and I held Linda's hands and said a brief prayer.

I told Lillian to call me if she needed me and left for home. This all took place late Friday afternoon.

The next morning, very early, I got a call from Lillian. Linda was now with God and her beloved Ed. She had passed on quietly during the night. Lillian sounded strong. I said I would be seeing her soon.

I got up, fixed some coffee, got the paper off the front porch and settled into my big chair. Before reading the paper, I pulled down my *Book of Common Prayer.* It fell

open to page 461, a place that is well worn. It is the page
on which a prayer I prayed many times is found. This is
a prayer for use by a sick person in the morning. It is so
magnificent I set it forth here:

This is another day, O Lord. I know not what it will bring forth,
but make me ready, Lord, for whatever it may be. If I am to stand
up, help me to stand bravely. If I am to sit still, help me to sit quietly.
If I am to lie low, help me do it patiently. And if I am to do nothing,
let me do it gallantly. Make these words more than words, and give
me the Spirit of Jesus. Amen.

If I did not know better, I would say that prayer was
written by Linda. Her spirit was healed. She now knows
the ultimate healing.

14. Urgency

You also must be ready; for the Son of man is coming at an unexpected hour.

Luke 12:40

Since that fateful year 1987, I continue to stay heavily involved with people with cancer. Likewise, my ministry to the jails and prisons is a big part of my life. Because of the events of that year, I find myself much closer to God. Somehow, he has led me through the trials and helped me come through without anger or bitterness. How can I give adequate thanks for such a portion of God's "holy grace"?

I have already said that sadness and uncertainty come over me at various times in varying degrees. If I take the time to think about it, I know I live under the ever-present threat of cancer. The wonderful story of the footprints in the sand hangs over my desk in my office. Briefly, it tells how a man had walked through a stormy life. His days were filled with turmoil, grief, and unrest. He believed in Jesus and tried to walk with him.

When he got to the end, he looked back and saw two sets of footprints in the sand representing his past. Jesus was at his side. At places, though, he saw only one set. "I thought you walked with me the whole way, Lord. What happened where there is only one set of footprints?"

"My precious child," Jesus answered, "Where you see only one set of footprints, you see where I carried you."

I know I was carried many times. There is no other explanation for my being here. My outlook I can attribute to only one thing, and that is God's grace. It is maintained by trying to follow his urgings to minister to others. Many times I do not feel like going to see someone who is close to death. Many times I do not want to devote an entire day

to a trip to the prison or a nice Sunday evening to ministering at the jail. They are not fun places to be.

It has never yet failed. When I force myself to go, I come
home blessed and filled with the Holy Spirit. I forget my
troubles, at least for a while. I do not want to sound at all
elitist about this. I guarantee this will happen to anyone.
It is as sure as the sun in the morning. Jesus tried to tell
us this same truth a dozen different ways. To gain life, we
must lose it. To be first, we must be last.

Those who know me best know it is hard for me to stay
tuned in to this way of life, but I keep trying. I know it is
the only way for me. When I venture back into the world,
I find it is not as great as it used to be. Once God has us,
he has us. When we try to get back into the old ways we
thought were so wonderful, we find they have lost their
luster. We cannot turn back. We must continue to follow
our Lord.

One friend of mine taught me another aspect of a disease
like cancer. He had cancer involving the lungs, about two
years ago. I first talked with him a year ago. It was clear
his spiritual understanding was non-Christian, almost cult-
ish. Since then, with great study and prayer, I feel he has
come to Jesus. I now see in him something that happens
occasionally. He had fully prepared himself to die.

Now, his cancer is in remission, if not gone altogether.
He has pain from some of the treatments, but his doctors
feel this will subside as he gets back on his feet. He is having
a hard time doing this. He was prepared to die. Now he must
prepare himself to live. Jesus Christ can help him do this.

One's first visit to the cancer floor of a big hospital is
grim. People dying of cancer, much like people dying of
most anything, are not pleasant to see. Most visitors have
the feeling of walking down death row. "How long are these
people going to live?" we want to know. Most are skin
and bones. To those who can detect it, the odor of death
permeates some of the rooms.

If one goes only once or twice to see a friend or loved
one, this first perception may be a lasting one. It is, I think,
what helps perpetuate the general notion that if a person
gets cancer, he or she is surely going to die. Let me remind

the reader, I was the most prejudiced person I knew when it came to cancer.

Much more is going on than we generally see on such a ward. A good percentage of the patients in the beds, who look so forlorn with all the tubes coming and going, are healthy, functioning people. These come into the hospital on a periodic basis to be given chemotherapy. It is easier for doctor and patient alike if it is administered in the hospital. Some have had cancer in remission for years. Soon after you have passed by the room, that person will have completed the treatment and be out of the hospital and back into the mainstream of life.

Another percentage are recuperating from successful surgery. After the appropriate stay they will be up and out, well on their way to a total cure. Yet others are in for various tests to determine just where they are in their cancer experience. Statistics now show us that 50 percent, or more, of people who get cancer will get well and live out a useful life. Five years is not really the magic number, but it is generally a yardstick in terms of a cure. Some doctors still use it. Others don't.

Admittedly, there is also a percentage of those patients on the cancer floor of any given hospital who will not leave alive. Let me suggest this is true of many patients on any floor of any hospital at any time. They will not last out the day. Many will die from a variety of diseases other than cancer.

Further, that is likewise the case with a percentage of people who will use the California freeways on any given day, or any other streets anywhere else. That is certainly true of passengers on a certain percentage of trains or planes. All are going to die some day. None of us knows when.

In many prisons in this country there is at least one stabbing a day. Many of these are fatal. Those prisoners do not know how long they are going to be here. Do we?

A timeworn question used by evangelists goes like this: "If you were to die tonight, do you know for certain you would go to Heaven? If not, do you know where you would go?" You can see how that opens the conversation to tell this person of Jesus Christ. It is a good question for us to ask ourselves from time to time. Once Christ has been accepted into one's heart, the answer is easy.

If my efforts have conveyed no other message, I strongly hope that one word comes through. That word is *urgency*. A reading of any of the Gospels should provoke at least a "what if?" If what is said there is true, Jesus is the only way. The amount of time any of us has left to make a decision for Christ is uncertain at best and unknown at worst. It is not so much a question of when Christ is coming back as it is how much longer each of us has to prepare for it. Whether we meet Christ by going to him in death or by his coming to us in the last days, we still have to be ready. Today, right this minute, could well be our last opportunity to ask him into our lives.

How can we wait? In my case I fiddled around playing the role of the Pharisee, thinking I knew Christ, until I was almost fifty years old. I did not know Christ. I knew what I wanted Christ to be. I was seduced by the crowd and the world. They told me a lie, one as old as Genesis. The great lie the serpent told Eve comes in many shapes and colors. We start believing we can be God. Learning the lesson that there is only one God, and that we are not God is often traumatic. There is room for only one God, and he has been there forever.

To know him, we must know Jesus, his Son. I may not like, understand, or believe that. Whether or not I believe something is not what makes it true. It is true whether I believe it or not. But I believe it with all my heart. All I had to do was say, "Your will, not mine, be done." Simple as that. God took it from there, some five years ago. Since then God has been working for good in my life. For that I offer my deepest thanks.

If you have not already invited Christ into your life, I would suggest pausing right now to pray a simple prayer. This is the best time to do it. Pray: "Dear Lord, I want to know you and your Son, Jesus Christ. Whatever the limits of my knowledge and understanding, I ask you into my heart. Forgive my sins and teach me your ways. In Christ's name, Amen." I know your life will change.

I have no way of knowing what this year will bring.

There will be joy, and there will be sadness, I am sure. There will be fun, and there will be drudgery. There will be sickness and health. Or, there may be death. That puts me in exactly the same boat with everyone else. No one knows. There is one thing I do know, however, that many do not. I know Jesus Christ is real and I know he is in my life in every way. This is the secret. This is how we can live with cancer or anything else that may befall us. With Christ we have life in illness and in death. That's the secret. If you prayed the above prayer, you know this, or you will before too long.

What a beautiful secret it is. What makes it even more beautiful is the fact it is an equal opportunity secret. It is a secret anyone can learn.

Lord God in heaven, please use me to spread your secret, to the end that all will know your Son, our Saviour, Jesus Christ. Amen.

Epilogue

In October, 1988, Ken Farnsworth underwent surgery for a relatively minor tumor in his right shoulder. The operation was a success and he is again cancer free. He continues his active life as a practicing attorney and lives in Fresno, California, with his wife Jan, to whom he has been happily married since May, 1988.

Whoever seeks to gain his life will lose it, but whoever loses his life will preserve it.

Luke 17:33